Twelve Steps

In Christ

Understanding the Biblical principles that enable us to overcome sin

RON HORDYK

Cover: Original Photo Thomas Bresson 2011

Twelve Steps In Christ
Copyright ©2016 Ron Hordyk

ISBN 978-1506-912-87-5 PRINT
ISBN 978-1506-903-71-2 EBOOK

LCCN 2016961156

December 2016

Published and Distributed by
First Edition Design Publishing, Inc.
P.O. Box 20217, Sarasota, FL 34276-3217
www.firsteditiondesignpublishing.com

ALL RIGHTS RESERVED. No part of this book publication may be reproduced, stored in a retrieval system, or transmitted in any form or by any means — electronic, mechanical, photo-copy, recording, or any other — except brief quotation in reviews, without the prior permission of the author or publisher.

To God,

Who—while I was a vile sinner—

saved me from sin, self, and Satan;

possessed me with the power of His presence;

elevated me to the position of a son;

and equipped me for the fulfilling of His purpose,

be the glory for ever and ever. Amen.

I give thanks for my family, friends,

and brothers and sisters in the Lord,

whom God used in my life

to shed the world while

being transformed into His image.

Permissions

Scriptures taken from the Holy Bible, **King James Version,** Public Domain. **(KJV)**

Scripture taken from the **New American Standard Bible**® Copyright © 1960,1962,1963,1968,1971,1972,1973,1975,1977,1995 by The Lockman Foundation. Used by permission. **(NASB)**

Scripture taken from the Holy Bible, **New International Version**. Copyright © 1973, 1978, 1984 International Bible Society. Zondervan Bible Publishers. **(NIV)**

Scripture taken from the **New King James Version**®. Copyright © 1982 by Thomas Nelson, Inc. Used by permission. All rights reserved. **(NKJV)**

Scripture quotations are from the **New Revised Standard Version Bible**, Copyright © 1989 the Division of Christian Education of the National Council of the Churches of Christ in the United States of America. Used by permission. All rights reserved. **(NRSV)**

Scripture taken from the Holy Bible, **New Living Translation**®. Copyright © 1998, 2004, 2007 by Tyndale House Foundation. Used by permission of Tyndale House Publishers Inc. Carol Stream, Illinois, 60188. All rights reserved worldwide. **(NLT)**

Scripture taken from the Holy Bible, **Today's New International Version**. TNIV Copyright © 1973, 1978, 1984 International Bible Society. Used by permission of the International Bible Society. All rights reserved worldwide. **(TNIV)**

Serenity Prayer

God grant me the serenity
To accept the things I cannot change,
The courage to change the things I can,
And the wisdom to know the difference.
Living one day at a time,
Enjoying one moment at a time;
Accepting hardship as a pathway to peace;
Taking, as Jesus did,
This sinful world as it is,
Not as I would have it;
Trusting that You will make all things right
If I surrender to Your will;
So that I may be reasonably happy in this life
And supremely happy with You forever in the next.
Amen

Reinhold Niebuhr.

Contents

Preface		viii
Step 1	Recognizing Our Limitations	1
Step 2	Reaching Beyond Ourselves	13
Step 3	Complete Surrender	25
Step 4	Assessing the Damage	39
Step 5	Facing the Facts	53
Step 6	Preparing for Change	69
Step 7	A Life of Humility	83
Step 8	Considering Past Harm	97
Step 9	Healing the Past	111
Step 10	Growing to Maturity	125
Step 11	Communion with God	139
Step 12	Sharing the Vision	153
Appendix	Romans 7	167

PREFACE

> *Therefore if anyone is in Christ, he is a new creation; the old is gone, the new has come!* (2 Co.5:17 NIV)

While I was living in Manhattan, New York, I met an older man at a Christian meeting. As we talked, we found that we agreed on many things, one of which was that man is dependent on God in order to change his life. He asked me if I worked the steps for a long time. I told him I did not know what he was talking about. I was only sharing the teachings from the Bible that helped me to live a holy life. I found out that this man went to Alcoholics Anonymous, and that its Twelve Step program was the basis for the man's beliefs.

Fifteen years later, I actually read the Twelve Steps and found them to be a complete presentation of how to deal with sin. The Twelve Steps were first founded on Biblical principles. Most people associate the Twelve Steps with Alcoholics Anonymous. Yet the Twelve Steps really began with Dr. Speer who divided the Sermon of the Mount into "The Four Absolutes": absolute honesty, absolute purity, absolute unselfishness, and absolute love. Frank Buchman then took these four absolutes as part of the normal Christian life. Frank applied them to himself, starting what was then known as the Oxford Group. When Frank went to China, he met a missionary Sam Shoemaker. Frank challenged Sam concerning his fear to share the Gospel, suggesting that sin might be the reason. Later Sam prayed, giving God his sins, his will, and his entire life. In 1926, Sam returned to the States to pastor Calvary Episcopal Church in New York City. Sam started a chapter of the Oxford Group. He developed Frank's principles into a "one to one" evangelism/discipleship program. Through Sam's principles, little prayer groups started throughout New York City, offering people the power to overcome their sin. The meetings consisted of personal sharing, public confession, prayer, Bible studies, and informal talks.

Preface

Bill Wilson started attending a meeting of the Oxford Group. The principles of the group empowered Bill Wilson to overcome alcohol addiction. Later Bill W. with Dr. Bob adapted the teachings of Sam's Oxford Group into Twelve Steps.[1] Alcoholics Anonymous was born with the Twelve Steps as its basic teachings. Later, the Twelve Steps were further adapted to reach out to other alcoholics without Christ. By totally removing the Bible from the Twelve Steps, they kept the structure but removed its power: the presence of God. It was in the later editions of the "Big Book" that we find the Twelve Steps being changed to "god as you understand him." AA has removed itself from its Christian roots to which it owes its success. God never told us to build big groups for Him nor to form deep theological arguments. He told us to follow Jesus in simple obedience and to make disciples who would do the same.

This book is written in simple English for the addict living on the street whose abuses may have affected his ability to think. The purpose of this book is to look at the original Biblical teachings that formed the foundation of the Twelve Step program. Many Christians have used the Twelve Steps without realizing its Christian origin. Through the lessons of this book, we will reunite the steps with the Bible and thereby release the power of God to permanently change lives. This collection of lessons is written also for new Christians who have a relationship with Jesus Christ. These lessons teach the basic principles of overcoming habitual sin. In the following pages, we will look at each of the twelve steps and the Scriptures given to support their importance. My hope is that the Church will embrace these neglected truths and may once again receive the holiness that Christ purchased for it. My prayer is that many in the Church who suffer from habitual sin will be freed to experience the abundant life that God promises to His people.

---

1. Alcoholics Anonymous Comes of Age, 1957 p.199

Step 1

Recognizing Our Limitations

Step 1 We recognize our inability to overcome sin by our own efforts—that we are born as slaves to sin.

All Have Sinned

In the first step, we focus on an uncommon topic: brokenness. People must be broken before they can become Christians. A broken person sees his life as hopeless and helpless. The Bible tells a story of a prodigal son. The son was selfish. He demanded his inheritance before his father died. Then, he left home with his things. He wasted his life in worldly pleasures and soon had no money left. With no other choice, the son worked on a pig farm. His life was out of control:

> And **he would gladly have filled his stomach with the pods that the swine ate,** and no one gave him anything. (Lk.15:16 NKJV)

The prodigal son had run out of money, friends, and answers. He was broken because he had no way out of his sin. In the same way, I was broken because I could not stop my sin. I still did those things that I hated doing. In Romans 7:7-25, Paul describes his life before he was a Christian:

> *I know that nothing good lives in me,* that is, **in my sinful nature**. For I have **the desire to do what is good,** but **I cannot carry it out.** For what I do is not the good I want to do; no, **the evil I do not want to do—this I keep on doing.** Now if I do what I do not want to do, it is no longer I who do it, but **it is sin living in me that does it.** (Ro.7:18-20 NIV)

Before Paul was a Christian, he was broken. Paul wanted to do good things; but he could not do good things. He always did the evil things that he hated. Paul's life was out of his control.

When everything seems wrong in your life, you feel better when you compare your life to the lives of others. You can usually find someone who is worse than yourself to make you feel better. An example would be like someone who competes in the long jump. He may not be able to jump far, but he can always find someone with one leg whom he can out-jump. The Bible teaches us:

> Oh, don't worry; we wouldn't dare say that we are as wonderful as these other men who tell you how important they are! **But they are only comparing themselves with each other, using themselves as the standard of measurement.** How ignorant! (2Co.10:12 NLT)

Even though you are better than other people, you are still not a perfect person. For example, a second-rate athlete competing in the long jump may not be able to jump very far, but he knows that he can jump further than someone with one leg. If you were standing on the edge of the Grand Canyon with a one-legged person, you would be able to jump further than he could, but the other side is a mile away. If both of you jumped, neither of you would reach the other side. You would both fall into the Grand Canyon and die. Jumping across the Grand Canyon is like trying to reach God by your own efforts. God is holy—absolutely perfect. The holy God is on one side of the canyon, and sinful man is on the other side. Man's goodness will never allow him to reach God. The Bible teaches:

> Pursue peace with all people, and **holiness, without which no one will see the Lord**. (He.12:14 NKJV)

God is perfect, and sin is imperfection. The perfect God cannot allow imperfect people into heaven. If he did, heaven would be no better than earth. God considers all sins to be equally wrong. From God's point of view, there are no big or little sins. Stealing a cookie is just as bad as stealing a car or someone's wife:

> For whoever keeps the whole law and yet stumbles at just one point **is guilty of breaking all of it**. (Ja.2:10 NIV)

One sin makes us imperfect. One little sin will keep us from heaven:

> There is no difference: **For all have sinned, and come short of the glory of God**. (Ro.3:23 KJV)

No matter how much good we do, God will not let us into heaven. God does not forget our past sins when we do good things. For example, our good actions are like a white wedding dress. Our sin is like a black spot.

If a person stains a white wedding dress, the wedding dress is ruined. When we sin, we ruin all the good that we have done:

> For all of us have become like one who is unclean, and **all our righteous deeds are like a filthy garment**. (Isa.64:6 NASB)

People have always done more evil than good. At the beginning of history, God did not give people any laws. At that time, God described how evil people were:

> The LORD saw how great man's wickedness on the earth had become, and that **every inclination** of the thoughts of his heart was **only** evil **all the time**. The LORD was grieved that he had made man on the earth, and his heart was filled with pain. (Ge.6:5-6 NIV)

God was very upset because people only thought about evil all the time. During the next 2000 years, God gave His people a set of laws. Now, God's people would know when they disobeyed God. But they still did not obey Him. At this time, Solomon described how the people behaved toward God:

> "**When** they sin against You (**for there is no one who does not sin**), and You become angry with them . . . ." (1Ki.8:46 NKJV; 2Ch.6:36)

The word *when* means that everyone still sinned. Again, God described the human heart at this time:

> The **heart is deceitful** above all things, and **desperately wicked**: who can know it? (Jer.17:9 NKJV)

After Jesus rose from the grave, God described non-Christians:

> Well then, should we conclude that we Jews are better than others? No, not at all, for we have already shown that **all people**, whether Jews or Gentiles, **are under the power of sin**. As the Scriptures say, "**No one** is righteous—**not even one**. **No one** is truly wise; **no one** is seeking God. **All** have turned away; **all** have become useless. **No one** does good, **not a single one**." (Ro.3:9-12 NLT)

At this time, all non-Christians still disobeyed God. No one lived to please God. Look around. Today, people are no different. We must conclude that everyone sins. People are not perfect. Therefore, non-Christians will not live with God in heaven:

> **All of us** also lived among them at one time, **gratifying the cravings of our sinful nature and following its desires and thoughts**. Like the rest, we **were** by nature objects of wrath. (Eph.2:3 NIV)

THE PURPOSE OF THE LAW

Everyone has disobeyed God. Some people hate the bad things that they do. So why do they still do bad things? Some people want to do good things. Then why don't they do good things? Something makes people act differently than they want to. The Bible teaches us that sin is not just an action. Sin is a power that controls us. Many people say that **they** decide what **they** want to do. However, some people hate their actions, but they cannot stop doing them. Why can't they stop their actions? They can't stop because they are slaves to sin:

> Truly, truly, I say to you, **everyone who commits sin is the slave of sin**.
> (Jn.8:34 NASB)

God gave us the Law to teach us that we are slaves to sin. Once we learn God's Law, we realize that we have disobeyed it. Hence, we know that we are sinners:

> For "no human being will be justified in his sight" by deeds prescribed by the law, **for through the law comes the knowledge of sin**.
> (Ro.3:20 NRSV)

When I learned that God required me to obey His Law, I tried to obey it. But I couldn't stop my sinful actions. Slowly, I realized that sin deceived me. I always thought that I chose my actions. But all that time, sin controlled me:

> **Indeed I would not have know what sin was except through the law**. For I would not have known what coveting really was if the law had not said, "Do not covet." **But sin, seizing the opportunity** afforded by the commandment, **produced in me every kind** of covetous desire.
> (Ro.7:7-8 NIV)

Sin controls our desires. Hence, we always choose to disobey God. God's Law shows us that sin is a power:

> **Apart from the law sin lies dead. I was once alive** apart from the law, but when the commandment came, **sin revived and I died**, and the very commandment that promised life **proved to be death to me**. For **sin, seizing** an opportunity in the commandment, **deceived me** and through it **killed me**.
> (Ro.7:8-10 NRSV)

The Law taught me what sin was when it told me not to do something. The Law made me choose. I could either obey God or disobey God. The power of sin influenced me, and I disobeyed God by doing evil. The Law gives sin more power because the Law forces everyone to make a choice:

> **The power of sin is the law.** (1Co.15:56 NRSV)

The Law gives sin power. For example, a father takes his son to a friend's farm, and the farm has a fish pond. The father tells his son to stay away from the pond. This command makes the boy curious about the pond. Suddenly, he wants it. If the child did not know about the pond, sin could not influence him to disobey. Likewise, if we do not know God's Law, sin cannot influence us to disobey it. Therefore, the Law increases our sin because every command gives us the knowledge of evil and forces us to make a choice. And, sin uses these choices to make us disobey God:

> The law was added **so that the trespass might increase.** (Ro.5:20 NIV)

The Law reveals that sin controls us. However, the Law never helps us do good. The Law warned us that God will judge us:

> For **all who have sinned without the Law will also perish** without the Law, and **all who have sinned under the Law will be judged** by the Law. (Ro.2:12 NASB)

God did not expect the Law to stop our sin or to help us obey:

> I do not treat the grace of God as meaningless. For **if keeping the law could make us right with God, then there was no need for Christ to die**. (Ga.2:21 NIV)

Rather, God gave us the Law to teach us that we are sinners and need help:

> For we know that **the Law is spiritual**, but I am of flesh, **sold into bondage to sin.** For **what I am doing, I do not understand; for I am not practicing what I would like to do**, but **I am doing the very thing I hate**. But **if I do the very thing I do not want to do**, I agree with the Law, confessing that <u>the Law is good</u>. So now, no longer am I the one doing it, but **sin which dwells in me.** (Ro.7:14-17 NASB)

The Law shows us that we are powerless against sin:

> But the Scripture declares that **the whole world is a prisoner of sin**, so that what was promised, being given through faith in Jesus Christ, might be given to those who believe. Before this faith came, **we were held prisoners by the law**, locked up until faith should be revealed. So **the law was put in charge to lead us to Christ** that we might be justified by faith. (Ga.3:22-24 NIV)

We must realize that we are slaves of sin, or we will never look for help. We might think that we do what we desire. But, the Law proves that sin controls us. Therefore, we cannot help ourselves, for without Christ, we are powerless over sin.

SIN'S DECEPTION

Why does sin control us? Sin controls us because of our sinful nature. Every person is born with a sinful nature:

> Surely **I was sinful at birth,** sinful **from the time my mother conceived me.** (Ps.51:5 NIV)

People do not sin and then get a sinful nature. Rather, people sin because they have a sinful nature. Our sinful nature makes us want to disobey God. When we were young, our parents did not teach us to sin. We naturally desired to sin:

> **These wicked people are born sinners;** even **from birth they have lied and gone their own way.** (Ps.58:3 NLT)

Babies are naturally selfish and sinful. For example, after a baby learns to roll over, he tries to roll over whenever his mother changes his diaper. The baby has learned to disobey his mother before he is one year old. According to the Bible, all people are inclined to sin because of their sinful nature:

> And **I know that nothing good lives in me**, that is, **in my sinful nature.** I **want to** do what is right, **but I can't.** **I want to** do what is good, **but I don't.** **I don't want to** do what is wrong, **but I do it anyway.** But if I do what I don't want to do, I am not really the one doing wrong; **it is sin living in me that does it.** (Ro.7:18-20 NLT)

You and I struggle with different sins because as people we are different. For example, I might struggle with drinking alcohol, but you don't. You might struggle with gambling, but I don't. Some sins control you, and other sins control me. However, everyone struggles with at least one sin:

> Therefore we also, since we are surrounded by so great a cloud of witnesses, let us lay aside every weight, and **the sin which so easily ensnares us**, and let us run with endurance the race that is set before us, (He.12:1 NKJV)

What is the sin that you struggle with? Finish this sentence: "My life would really come together if only I could. . . ." You might struggle with alcohol, gambling, cigarettes, drugs, sex, violence, laziness, or whatever. Every person has at least one sin which controls him:

> They promise them freedom, but they themselves are slaves of corruption; **for people are slaves to whatever masters them**.
> (2Pe.2:19 NRSV)

My friend's brother had a problem with drinking alcohol. When I asked about his brother's drinking, my friend said, "My brother just likes beer." This was not true. He could not stop at one drink because his sinful nature caused him to drink to excess. He did not control his drinking, but his drinking controlled him. Therefore, people sin because their sinful nature makes them a slave of a sin.

We like to think that we can choose freely between good and evil; however, we give in to evil and do bad things. After some time, when we try to stop our sins, we can't. Hence, we learn that our desire for evil is stronger than our desire to do good. Throughout our lives, without Christ, we are never free to choose good. Rather, our sinful nature makes us desire evil things. We are deceived:

> **For we also once were** foolish ourselves, **disobedient, <u>deceived</u>, enslaved to various lusts and pleasures**, spending our life in malice and envy, hateful, hating one another.
> (Ti.3:3 NASB)

We do not realize that our sinful nature inclines us to sin. We are self-deceived. We always do certain sins, but we cannot understand why. We are blind to our addiction. Therefore, we defend our wrong actions:

> This includes you who were once far away from God. **You were his enemies, separated from him by your evil thoughts and actions**.
> (Co.1:21 NLT)

We do not believe that we have a problem. However, we are the problem because our nature desires sin:

> **All of us** used to live that way, **following the passionate desires and inclinations of our sinful nature**. By our very nature we were subject to God's anger, just like everyone else.
> (Eph 2:3 NLT)

We naturally oppose God. For example, God asked us to love our neighbor. However, we are inclined to ignore our neighbor because of our sinful nature:

> *For the sinful nature desires what is contrary to the Spirit, and the Spirit what is contrary to the sinful nature. They are in conflict with each other, **so that you do not do what you want**.* (Ga.5:17 NIV)

We must realize that our nature rebels against God:

> ***Those who live according to the <u>sinful nature</u> have their minds set on what that nature desires**; but those who live in accordance with the Spirit have their minds set on what the Spirit desires. The mind of sinful man is death, but the mind controlled by the Spirit is life and peace;* **the sinful mind is hostile to God. It does not submit to God's law, nor can it do so.** *Those <u>**controlled by the sinful nature**</u> cannot please God.* (Ro.8:5-8 NIV)

When God commands us to do good, we naturally want to disobey. We cannot stop our sinful actions. Our nature inclines us to disobey God. Our sinful nature is part of who we are. Therefore, we cannot manage our lives:

> *For when **we were controlled by the sinful nature**, the sinful passions aroused by the law were at work in our bodies, so that **we bore fruit for death**.* (Ro 7:5 NIV)

We need to admit that we sin. Everyone struggles with at least one sin:

> ***If we say that we have no sin**, we are deceiving ourselves and the truth is not in us.* (1Jn.1:8 NASB)

When we agree that we cannot manage our lives, then we can begin to seek help. Could I save myself? No! When I knew I could not stop my sin, I asked God for help:

> ***When we were utterly helpless, Christ came at just the right time and died for us** sinners. Now, most people would not be willing to die for an upright person, though someone might perhaps be willing to die for a person who is especially good. But God showed his great love for us by sending **Christ to die for us while we were still sinners**.* (Ro.5:6-8 NLT)

Are we aware that we are slaves to our sin? Do we know that we cannot free ourselves? We are powerless. We cannot stop our sins. We must realize that we cannot manage our lives. Only then will we seek help and find hope:

> *"**For when I am weak**, then I am strong."* (2Co.12:10 NKJV)

SPIRITUAL HEART DISEASE

Only when we realize that we are sick, will we go to the doctor. We describe our symptoms to the doctor. However, we will not get better until the doctor finds and fixes the problems in our bodies. God is like a doctor. In Exodus 4-14, God explains why Pharaoh did evil:

> Why do you <u>harden your hearts</u> as the Egyptians and Pharaoh did?
> (1Sa.6:6 NIV)

Sin controlled and hardened Pharaoh's heart. Therefore, Pharaoh disobeyed God. Today, we are just like Pharaoh. We disobey God because sin controls our hearts. We have wicked hearts:

> <u>The heart</u> is deceitful above all things, and desperately wicked: who can know it? (Jer.17:9 KJV)

We think with our minds, but our hearts control our thoughts:

> For **as he thinks in his heart, so is he.** (Pr.23:7 NKJV)

Our hearts control our thoughts, and our thoughts control our actions. Therefore, our wicked hearts control what we say and do:

> The good man out of **the good treasure of his heart** brings forth what is good; and the evil man out of the evil treasure brings forth what is evil; **for his mouth speaks from that which fills his heart**. (Lk.6:45 NASB)

Because of our wicked hearts, we think bad thoughts. Because of our wicked thoughts, we say and do bad things. We sin because of our wicked hearts:

> Anything you eat passes through the stomach and then goes into the sewer. But **the words you speak come from the heart**—that's what defiles you. **For from the heart come evil thoughts**, murder, adultery, all sexual immorality, theft, lying, and slander. **These are what defile you.** Eating with unwashed hands will never defile you. (Mt.15:17-20 NLT)

In the Bible, David linked his sin to his wicked heart. For example, after David slept with another man's wife, he asked God for a new heart. David knew that he had sinned because of his wicked heart:

> **Create in me a clean heart**, O God, and **put a new and right spirit** within me. (Ps.51:10 NRSV)

As long as we have a wicked heart, we cannot stop our sins. We need to get rid of our wicked heart:

> Take care, brothers and sisters, **that none of you may have an evil, unbelieving heart that turns away from the living God.**

(He.3:12 NRSV)

Therefore, we must recognize our inability to overcome sin by our own efforts—that we are born as slaves to sin. We need to understand the following steps that deal with the power of sin, our sinful nature, and our wicked heart.

For Further Thought:

When I cannot stop my sins, I...

1. What is brokenness?

2. Why is it a bad idea to compare ourselves with others?

3. Why are there no big or little sins in God's eyes?

4. Why did God give us the Law?

5. How did sin get power over us?

6. What is the sinful nature?

7. According to the Bible, are we free to choose between good and evil?

8. Describe your heart. How does your heart make you act?

Memory Verse:
There is no difference, for all have sinned, and fall short of the glory of God.
Romans 3:23 NIV

NOTES:

Step 2

Reaching Beyond Ourselves

Step 2 *We believe that Jesus, Who is greater than we are, can fulfill His promise to transform our lives.*

God Is Just

God is just, and a just person is fair. To be fair, God must punish us according to His Law because we have disobeyed His Law. We cannot hide our sins. God knows everything about us and sees all our sin:

> O LORD, **You have searched me and known me**. You know **when I sit down** and **when I rise up**; You **understand my thought** from afar. You **scrutinize my path** and **my lying down**, And are **intimately acquainted with all my ways**. Even before there is **a word on my tongue**, Behold, O LORD, You know it all. (Ps.139:1-4 NASB)

Since God knows everything, He can judge us without witnesses:

> For I recognize my rebellion; **it haunts me day and night**. Against you, and you alone, have **I sinned; I have done what is evil in your sight**. You will be proved right in what you say, and **your judgment against me is just**. (Ps.51:3-5 NLT)

Because God has never sinned, He is holy (perfect). God hates sin and, therefore, cannot live with us because of our sinful nature:

> For You are not a God **who takes pleasure in wickedness**; **No evil dwells with You**. The boastful shall not stand before Your eyes; **You hate all who do iniquity**. (Ps.5:4-5 NASB)

Once a person dies, God will judge him. Because God is fair (just), He must punish everyone according to His Law:

> **For God does not show favoritism**. **All who sin** apart from the law will also **perish** apart from the law, and **all who sin** under the law will be **judged** by the law. (Ro.2:11-12 NIV)

God judges our sinful nature by our actions:

> God "will give to each person according to what he has done." To those who by persistence in doing good seek glory, honor and immortality, he will give eternal life. But for those **who are self-seeking and who reject the truth and follow evil,** there will be wrath and anger.
> (Ro.2:6-8 NIV; Mt 16:27; 2Co 5:10; 1Pe. 4:17)

When we do good things, it does not cancel out our bad actions. If we break one of God's laws, we are sinners, and God must punish us:

> But **God shows his anger from heaven against all sinful, wicked people** who suppress the truth by their wickedness. (Ro.1:18 NLT)

God is just (fair). Therefore, He judges us by our actions. Because of our sinful actions, God must punish us forever in the lake of fire.

GOD IS LOVE

God must punish all of us for our sin because He is just. But God is also love:

> **God is love.** (1Jn.4:16 NKJV; 4:8; Ps.86:5)

Because God is love, He wants to forgive us. How can God be both loving and just toward us? Since God is the judge, only He can find a way to be both loving and just:

> I, yes **I,** am the LORD, and there is no other Savior. (Isa.43:11 NLT)

God's answer was to come to the earth as a man. His name was Jesus. Jesus lived a perfect life. He did not deserve to die and be punished for sins that He did not commit. Nonetheless, Jesus took our punishment upon Himself when He let evil men kill Him. Through His death on a cross, Jesus paid the penalty for our sins. Sins are individual acts. They can be listed, added up, and totaled. God knows exactly how many sins we have committed up to this moment because sins are finite. Perfection on the other hand is an absolute. Once we are perfect, we cannot become more perfect. As an absolute, perfection is infinite. Therefore, the death of one infinitely perfect man, Jesus, can pay for the total sins of humanity because sins are finite. By paying for our sins with His own life, God showed His love for us:

> **But God proves his love for us** in that while we still were sinners Christ died for us. (Ro.5:8 NLT)

The penalty for our sins is more than death. The final penalty for sin is hell. When Jesus died, He went down into hell (the center of the earth), where He fully paid our penalty. But because He is God, hell could not keep Him. Therefore, Jesus rose from the dead:

> For as Jonah was three days and three nights in the belly of a huge fish, so **the Son of Man** will be three days and three nights **in the heart of the earth**. (Mt.12:40 NIV; Eph.4:9; Ac.2:27)

Through Jesus, God can be both just and loving toward us. Because God is just, someone must pay the penalty for our sins. Because God is love, Jesus paid the penalty:

> For God **so loved the world** that he gave his one and only Son, that whoever believes in him shall not perish but have eternal life.
> (Jn.3:16 NIV)

God does not love the world with its sin. Rather, He loved the world 2000 years ago when He died for our sins. We must believe that Jesus paid our penalty and ask Him to forgive our sins. Otherwise, God will have to punish us. Some people do not believe that Jesus died for their sins. If others refuse to ask Jesus to pay their penalty, God will punish them for their own sins:

> **He who believes in the Son has eternal life**; but he who does not obey the Son will not see life, **but the wrath of God abides on him."**
> (Jn.3:36 NASB)

We naturally go to hell because we have sinned:

> Those who believe in him are not condemned; but **those who do not believe are condemned <u>already</u>**, because they have not believed in the name of the only Son of God. (Jn.3:18 NRSV)

Jesus saves people from hell when they ask Him to forgive their sins:

> They tell how you turned to God from idols to serve the living and true God, and to wait for his Son from heaven, whom he raised from the dead—
> **Jesus, who rescues us from the coming wrath**.
> (1Th.1:9-10 NIV)

There is no other way for us to avoid hell. Jesus is our only hope:

> For **while we were still helpless**, at the right time **Christ died for the ungodly**. (Ro 5:6 NASB)

Therefore, because God is loving and just, He lovingly died in our place. If we trust in Jesus, we do not have to go to hell.

JESUS WAS FULLY MAN

The Holy Spirit came upon Mary, and she became pregnant by the power of God. Because Jesus' mother was fully human, Jesus was a man:

> This is how Jesus the Messiah was born. **His mother, Mary**, was engaged to be married to Joseph. But before the marriage took place, **while she was still a virgin, she became pregnant through the power of the Holy Spirit**. (Mt.1:18 NLT)

Jesus experienced childhood and youth:

> **The Child continued to grow and become strong**, increasing in wisdom; and the grace of God was upon Him. Now His parents went to Jerusalem every year at the Feast of the Passover. **And when He became twelve**, they went up there according to the custom of the Feast. (Lk.2:40-42 NASB)

Because Jesus was a man, He had to obey God's Law:

> But when the time had fully come, God sent **his Son, born of a woman, born under law,** to redeem those under law, that we might receive the full rights of sons. (Ga.4:4-5 NIV)

The New Testament calls Jesus "the Son of Man" 84 times:

> No one has ascended into heaven except the one who descended from heaven, the Son of Man. And just as Moses lifted up the serpent in the wilderness, so must **the Son of Man be lifted up**, that whoever believes in him may have eternal life. (Jn.3:13-15 NRSV)

Jesus experienced life. He was hungry at times. Jesus cried when His friend died. Men hated Jesus and wanted to kill Him. Jesus experienced many of the same feelings that we feel:

> Therefore **he had to become like his brothers and sisters in every respect**, so that he might be a merciful and faithful high priest in the service of God, to make a sacrifice of atonement for the sins of the people. **Because he himself was tested** by what he suffered, **he is able to help those who are being tested**. (He.2:17-18 NLT)

Jesus was tempted by Satan just as we are. Jesus knows that it is hard to turn away from sin. But Jesus never gave in to sin:

> This High Priest of ours understands our weaknesses, for **he faced all of the same testings we do, yet he did not sin.** So let us come boldly to the throne of our gracious God. There we will receive his mercy, and **we will find grace to help us when we need it most.** (He.4:15-16 NLT)

Since people sinned, only a perfect person could die in our place. Jesus lived for 33 years on the earth as a man. Therefore, Jesus knows what it is like to be tempted, but He had the strength not to sin. From experience, He knows what we all go through.

JESUS IS FULLY GOD

The Bible states that Jesus' mother gave birth to Him while she was still a virgin. For Jesus was conceived by God:

> Mary said to the angel, "How can this be, **since I am a virgin**?" The angel said to her, "**The Holy Spirit will come upon you**, and the **power of the Most High** will overshadow you; therefore the child to be born will be holy; he will be **called Son of God**. (Lk.1:34-35 NRSV)

Twice God's voice from heaven said that Jesus was His Son:

> And a voice from heaven said, "**This is my Son**, whom I love; with him I am well pleased." (Mt.3:17 NIV; Mt.17:5)

Jesus humbled Himself and assumed a relationship of a Son to a Father when He came down to earth. In every way, Jesus was like God because He was God:

> Your attitude should be the same as that of Christ Jesus: Who, **being in very nature God**, did not consider **equality with God** something to be grasped, but made himself nothing, taking the very nature of a servant, being made in human likeness. (Php.2:5-7 NIV; Co.2:9)

Jesus talked and acted like God. Jesus was like God in all areas of life:

> The Son is the radiance of God's glory and **the exact representation of his being**, sustaining all things by his powerful word. After he had provided purification for sins, he sat down at the right hand of the Majesty in heaven. (He.1:3 NIV)

Jesus was not only God's Son. Jesus was God:

> We look forward with hope to that wonderful day **when the glory of our great God and Savior, Jesus** *Christ, will be revealed.* He gave his life **to free us from every kind of sin, to cleanse us**, *and to make us his very own people, totally committed to doing good deeds.*
>
> (Ti.2:13-14 NLT; Jn.1:1; 1Jn.5:20; Ro 9:5; Jn.20:28; Jn.14:9)

Because Jesus was a man, Satan tempted Jesus like Satan tempts us. (When Satan tempts us, he tries to make us sin.) However, Jesus was also God, and as God, Jesus was holy (perfect). Jesus did not sin when Satan tempted Him because He shared God's divine nature:

> *"For we do not have a high priest who is unable to sympathize with our weaknesses, but* **we have one who has been tempted in every way, just as we are—yet was without sin.***"* (He.4:15 NIV)

Jesus felt the pull of sin, but He did not sin. Therefore, Jesus could use His death as a payment for our sins:

> *For* **God made Christ, who never sinned, to be the offering for our sin**, *so that we could be made right with God through Christ.*
>
> (2Co.5:21 NLT)

Jesus came to earth to die for our sins:

> *For* **Christ also suffered for sins once for all, the righteous for the unrighteous**, *in order to bring you to God. He was put to death in the flesh, but made alive in the spirit.* (1Pe.3:18 NRSV)

According to the Bible, Jesus' death could pay the penalty of sin for every person who ever lived:

> *He himself is the sacrifice that atones for our sins—***and not only our sins but the sins of all the world.*** (1Jn.2:2 NLT)

Since Jesus is God, He did not sin. Therefore, because He was a sinless man, His death could pay the penalty for all sins. Now because of Jesus, everyone who believes in Him can go to heaven:

> *Jesus *said to him, "***I am the way***, and the truth, and the life;* **no one comes to the Father but through Me.*** (Jn.14:6 NASB)

CHRIST CAN HELP US

Jesus' death is important. But Jesus' resurrection is also important. Jesus died on a cross to pay the penalty for our sins and to save us from hell. But Jesus also rose from the dead to free us from a life of slavery to sin:

> *If there is no resurrection of the dead, then not even Christ has been raised. And if Christ has not been raised, **our preaching is useless and so is your faith**.... For if the dead are not raised, then Christ has not been raised either. And if Christ has not been raised, **your faith is futile; you are still in your sins**. Then those also **who have fallen asleep in Christ are lost**.* (1Co.15:13-18 NIV)

If Jesus only died, He could not help us overcome our sins. Since Jesus rose from the dead and lives today, He can help us overcome sin:

> *Therefore **he is able to <u>save completely</u>** those who come to God through him, because **he always lives to intercede for them**.* (He.7:25 NIV)

Are you tempted? Jesus knows how to help when we are tempted because He was tempted and He did not sin:

> *For we do not have a high priest who cannot sympathize with our weaknesses, but One **who has been tempted in all things as we are, yet without sin**. Therefore let us draw near with confidence to the throne of grace, so that we may receive mercy and **find grace to help in time of need**.* (He.4:15-16 NASB)

Do you suffer from a wicked heart? Jesus lives to heal our wicked hearts and fix our messed up lives:

> *He Himself bore our sins in His body on the cross, so that **we might die to sin and live to righteousness**; for **by His wounds you were healed**.* (1Pe.2:24 NASB)

Do you feel like a lost cause? Jesus lives to save the lost:

> *Jesus said to him, "Today salvation has come to this house, because he too is a son of Abraham. For **the Son of Man came to seek out and to save the lost**."* (Lk.19:9-10 NRSV)

Do you feel powerless to reach out to God? God is reaching out to us through Jesus:

> *You see, at just the right time, **when we were still powerless, Christ died for the ungodly**.* (Ro.5:6-8 NIV)

Do you feel unworthy because of your sins? Jesus lives to free us from the shame of our sins:

> *Jesus answered them, "Most assuredly, I say to you, whoever commits sin is a slave of sin. Therefore if **the Son makes you free, you shall be free indeed**.* (Jn.8:34, 36 NKJV)

Do you feel weighed down by our past actions? Do you feel tired of sin? Jesus lives to give us rest:

> *"Come to me, **all you that are weary and are carrying heavy burdens**, and **I will give you rest**.* (Mt.11:28-29 NRSV)

Do you feel worthless and tired of life? Jesus gives us a reason to live:

> *God, who has saved us and called us to a holy life— **not because of anything we have done but because of his own purpose** and grace.* (2Ti.1:9 NIV)

We are not the answer to our problems and feelings. Christ is the answer. I know because I was there. Jesus said:

> *I came that they may **have life**, and **have it abundantly**.* (Jn.10:10 NASB)

Therefore, we must reach beyond ourselves to Christ:

> ***There is salvation in no one else**; for there is no other name under heaven that has been given among men by which we must be saved."* (Ac.4:12 NASB)

Since Jesus lives, He can wipe clean the past, help us moment by moment, and restore us to wholeness!

JESUS IS ALWAYS THERE

At times, we really struggle with sin. We need a friend to help us through those times, but no one person can be with us at all times. When we struggle the most with sin, we often find ourselves alone. If we believe in Jesus, we will never be alone. God said to those who believe in Jesus:

> *For He Himself has said, **"I will never leave you nor forsake you."*** (He.13:5 NKJV)

The Holy Spirit is the Spirit of God and Jesus. As we said before, Jesus is God:

> *You, however, are controlled not by the sinful nature but by the Spirit, if the **Spirit of God** **lives in you**. And if anyone does not have the **Spirit of Christ**, he does not belong to Christ.* (Ro.8:9 NIV)

We need to reach beyond ourselves and invite Jesus Christ to live in us:

> *Listen! I am standing at the door, knocking; **if you hear my voice and open the door, I will come in to you** and eat with you, and you with me.* (Re 3:20 NRSV)

If we invite Jesus into our lives, God will live within us:

> Jesus answered and said to him, "If anyone loves Me, he will keep My word; and **My Father will love him**, and **We will <u>come to him</u> and make <u>Our home with him</u>.**" (Jn.14:23 NKJV)

Unlike a guest, God will not enter us and then leave us later. When God lives in us, His Holy Spirit will be in us forever:

> And I will ask the Father, and he will give you **another Counselor to be with you <u>for ever</u>—the Spirit of truth**. . . . **But you know him, for he lives with you and will be in you.** (Jn.14: 16-17 NIV)

Jesus Christ can live in us through His Holy Spirit. Jesus has promised that He will always be with Christians:

> Go therefore and **make disciples of all nations**, baptizing them in the name of the Father and of the Son and of the Holy Spirit, and teaching them to obey everything that I have commanded you. And remember**, I am with you always,** to the end of the age. (Mt.28:19-20 NRSV)

Because Jesus lives in Christians forever, He helps them to stop sinning so that Christians do not continue in their sins:

> And you know that **Jesus came to take away our sins**, and there is no sin in him. **Anyone who continues to live in him will not sin**. But **anyone who keeps on sinning does not know him or understand who he is.** (1Jn.3:5-6 NLT)

If the Holy Spirit lives in us, He will change our lives. Our lives will become more like Christ's life. We cannot change ourselves, only Christ can make a difference:

> "I am the vine, you are the branches. **He who abides in Me, and I in him**, bears much fruit; **for without Me you can do nothing**. (Jn.15:5 NKJV)

Because Christ lives in Christians and gives them strength, Christians can feel weak and still not sin:

> **For when I am weak, then I am strong.** (2Co 12:10 NKJV)

No matter how a Christian feels, he still can refuse to sin. For the Holy Spirit gives strength to Christians:

> I pray that out of his glorious riches **he may strengthen you with power through his Spirit in your inner being**, so that Christ may dwell in your hearts through faith. (Eph.3:16-17 NIV)

Do not let anyone deceive you. Jesus went through everything that we go through. Therefore, God can restore us to wholeness. We must believe that Jesus paid the penalty for our sins. We must ask Jesus to forgive our sins, and ask the Holy Spirit to live in us. Then, the Holy Spirit will be with us forever. He will help us stop our sinning:

> *And the testimony is this, that God has given us eternal life, and this life is in His Son.* **He who has the Son has the life**; *he who does not have the Son of God does not have the life.* (Jn.5:11-12 NASB)

For Further Thought:

Every time I think about God, I feel...

1. How do you feel when someone does not get the penalty that he deserves?

2. Why doesn't God love the world with its sin?

3. How was Jesus the solution to God's justice and love?

4. Is it hard for you to believe that God loves you? Why?

5. Why is it important that Jesus was a man?

6. Why is it important that Jesus is God?

7. Why is it important to know that Jesus lives today?

8. Why is it important that Jesus promises to never leave you?

Memory Verse:
> *He himself bore our sins in his body on the tree, so that we might die to sins and live for righteousness; by his wounds you have been healed.*
> 1 Peter 2:24

NOTES:

Step 3

Complete Surrender

STEP 3 *We completely surrender our lives to Christ, asking Him to take control.*

Covenant

Because we know that we cannot manage our lives, we must believe in Jesus Christ and trust Him to fix our lives. If we really trust Christ, we will obey His commands. For we know that His commands are good for us. Therefore, we must turn our lives over to God. In other words, we must make Jesus our Lord (master).

Once we believe in Jesus, God offers us a covenant. A covenant is an agreement with a promise between God and man:

> **Repent, and be baptized every one of you** *in the name of Jesus Christ so that your sins may be forgiven; and you will receive the gift of the Holy Spirit. For* **the promise is for you, for your children, and for all** *who are far away, everyone whom the Lord our God calls to him.*
>
> (Ac.2:38-39 NRSV)

According to the covenant, God commands us to repent and be baptized. After we obey, God will forgive our sins and give us the Holy Spirit. You might think, "I don't like the deal!" Remember: we need Jesus to forgive our sins. Also, we need the Holy Spirit to help us stop our sins. If we believe these two facts, we will repent and be baptized. We deserve hell because of our sins. But because God loves us, He gave us this covenant. Therefore, God's covenant (agreement) is the only way that we can be made right with God. Through this covenant (repent and be baptized), we make Jesus the Lord of our lives.

REPENTANCE

In the covenant, God commands us to repent. If we do not repent, we will go to hell:

> *"But **unless you repent**, you too will all perish."* (Lk.13:3 NIV; 2Co.7:10)

We must experience repentance, or God will not forgive our sins:

> **Repent** *therefore, and* **turn to God** *so that your sins may be wiped out, so that times of refreshing may come from the presence of the Lord.*
> (Ac.3:19-20 NRSV)

When we experience repentance, we turn away from sin, turn toward God, and desire to please Him:

> *I have declared to **both Jews and Greeks** that they **must turn to God** in repentance and have faith in our Lord Jesus.* (Ac.20:21 NIV)

People naturally rebel against God. We want to sin because of our sinful nature. Hence, our desire to repent must come from God:

> *They glorified God, saying, "Then **God has also granted** to the Gentiles repentance to life."* (Ac.11:18 NKJV; 2Ti.2:25)

From this point on, I will assume that you have experienced repentance. **The word *repentance* means "to have a change of mind."** Repentance is the complete change of our mind's direction and purpose. When we experience repentance, God changes our minds. Before this change, our sinful nature controlled our minds. Consequently, we sinned on purpose. After we repent and are baptized, the Holy Spirit takes control of our minds, and we no longer rebel against God. Rather, we live to please Him:

> *Those who live according to the sinful nature have their minds set on what that nature desires; but **those who live in accordance with the Spirit have their minds set on what the Spirit desires**. The mind of sinful man is death, but **the mind controlled by the Spirit is life and peace**; the sinful mind is hostile to God. It does not submit to God's law, nor can it do so.* (Ro.8:5-7 NIV)

The Holy Spirit is Christ's Spirit. Because the Holy Spirit has taken control of our minds, we have Christ's mind:

> *"But **we** have **the mind of Christ**."* (1Co.2:16 NKJV)

If you put my wife's mind in my head, my wife's mind would control my body, and I would act like she does. My actions would change even though I would look the same. In the same way, when we repent and are baptized, we receive the Holy Spirit. At that time, we also receive the mind of Christ and begin to act like Him:

> But God's truth stands firm like a foundation stone with this inscription: "The LORD knows those who are his," and "**All who belong to the LORD must turn away from evil.**" (2Ti.2:19 NLT)

Because of Christ's mind, we stop our sins one at a time; and we become more holy. Our actions show whether or not we experienced repentance:

> I preached first to those in Damascus, then in Jerusalem and throughout all Judea, and also to the Gentiles, that **all must repent of their sins** and **turn to God**—and **prove they have changed by the good things they do.** (Ac.26:20 NLT)

We experience repentance only once, for God changes a person's mind only once. However, we repent throughout our Christian lives. The word *repent* is different than *repentance*. **The word *repent* means "to change one's mind."** For example, if I went into a store to buy a shirt but changed my mind, would I buy the shirt? No, because I changed my mind. As we learn about Christ, the Holy Spirit changes our minds about our actions. Then, we repent and turn away from our sinful actions. Think about the following example. Before a man was a Christian, He sold a car. But he did not tell the buyer that the car had engine problems. Later, the seller became a Christian. The Holy Spirit taught him that he lied to the buyer. He repented of his lying. Because of Christ, he no longer lies when he sell things. Throughout the years as the Holy Spirit changes our opinions about all things, we continue to turn away from our sins and act more and more like Christ:

> That is how we know we are living in him. **Those who say they live in God should live their lives as Jesus did.** (1Jn.2:5-6 NLT)

When we experience repentance, the Holy Spirit replaces God's Law. We no longer focus on obeying God's Law. Rather, we focus on the Holy Spirit, Who speaks to our minds. He tells us when we disobey God and what God wants us to do. The Holy Spirit always agrees with the Bible. He teaches us how to please God:

> "For this is the covenant that I will make with the house of Israel after those days, says the LORD: **I will put My laws in their mind and write them on their hearts**; and I will be their God, and they shall be My people. (He.8:10 NKJV)

Therefore, repentance leads to salvation. When we experience repentance, God changes our minds, and we no longer rebel against God. Rather, we live to please Him. Because we have Christ's mind, the Holy Spirit changes our thinking. He points out our sinful actions one at a time, and we repent. As a result, we act more and more like Christ:

> Therefore let us leave the **elementary teachings** about Christ and go on to maturity, **not laying again <u>the foundation of repentance</u> from acts that lead to death**. (He.6:1 NIV)

Therefore, all Christians have received the mind of Christ (repentance) and continue to change their actions (to daily repent) from sin to holiness.

BAPTISM

In the covenant, God commands us to do two things: repent and be baptized. When someone is baptized, he is put all the way under the water, an act in which he dies to self. Through baptism, we call on the name of the Lord Jesus:

> 'Now why do you delay? Get up and **be baptized**, and wash away your sins, <u>**calling**</u> **on His name**.' (Ac 22:16 NASB)

Baptism is the Biblical way that we call on the Lord Jesus:

> For there is no difference between Jew and Gentile- the same Lord is Lord of all and richly blesses all who call on Him, for, "Everyone who **calls on the name of the Lord <u>will be saved</u>**." (Ro.10:12-13 NIV)

The new covenant makes baptism necessary to be forgiven:

> And he said to them, "Go into all the world and proclaim the good news to the whole creation. **The one who believes and is baptized will be saved**; but the one who does not believe will be condemned. (Mk.16:15-16 NRSV)

Jesus commanded baptism for people who have come to believe in Him:

> Go therefore and make disciples of all nations, **baptizing them in the name of the Father and of the Son and of the Holy Spirit, and teaching them to obey everything** that I have commanded you. (Mt.20:19-20 NRSV)

Philip preached about Jesus to the Samaritans. When the Samaritans believed in Jesus, they were baptized:

> *When they believed Philip preaching* the good news about the kingdom of God and the name of Jesus Christ, **they were being baptized, men and women alike.** (Ac.8:12 NASB)

Paul baptized the Philippian jailer the same night he believed in Jesus:

> They replied, "Believe in the Lord Jesus, and you will be saved—you and your household." Then they spoke the word of the Lord to him and to all the others in his house. At that hour of the night the jailer took them and washed their wounds; **then immediately he and all his family were baptized.** (Ac.16:31-33 NIV)

The act of baptism alone will not save anyone. Only baptism in response to believing in Christ will save a person:

> For God loved the world so much that he gave his one and only Son, so **that everyone who believes in him will not perish but have eternal life.** (Jn.3:16 NLT)

Because we believe in Jesus, we will obey what He says. He commands us to repent and be baptized. When people truly believe in Jesus Christ, they will respond in repentance. Because they have received the mind of Christ, they will want to obey Jesus Christ in everything. If someone refuses to be baptized, he does not truly believe in Jesus Christ:

> So you see, faith by itself isn't enough. **Unless it produces good deeds, it is dead and useless. . .** You see, his faith and his actions worked together. **His actions made his faith complete. . .** So you see, **we are shown to be right with God by what we do, not by faith alone. . .** Just as the body is dead without breath, **so also faith is dead without good works.** (Ja.2:17, 22, 24 & 26 NLT)

If people believe something, their actions will change to match their belief. To believe and not obey what Jesus says is to have a faith like the demons:

> You believe that there is one God. You do well. **Even the demons believe—and tremble!** (Ja.2:19 NKJV)

Before we believed in Jesus Christ, we rebelled against God. Having experienced repentance, we now obey Jesus. Jesus commands that we be baptized. Jesus only saves those who obey Him:

> Although he was a Son, he learned obedience through what he suffered; and having been made perfect, **he became the source of eternal salvation for all who obey him.** (He.5:8-9 NRSV)

Baptism is the first command Jesus gave to Christians. However, baptism is not the only way that we obey Jesus Christ:

> I wrote for this reason: **to test you and to know whether you are obedient in everything.** (2Co 2:9 NRSV)

Obedience only in baptism is not enough; we must obey Jesus in everything:

> Peter, an apostle of Jesus Christ, To those who reside as aliens. . . **according to** the foreknowledge of God the Father, **by the** sanctifying work of the Spirit, **to obey Jesus Christ.** (1Pe.1:1-2 NASB)

Baptism is only the first step of our journey of life in Christ. But every journey must take that first step:

> **Corresponding to that, baptism now saves you**—not the removal of dirt from the flesh, but an appeal to God for a good conscience—**through the resurrection of Jesus Christ.** (1Pe.3:21 NASB)

In the covenant, God commands that we repent and be baptized. Therefore, we must experience repentance and baptism before we are saved.

THE OLD IS GONE

In our baptism, we ended our old life of sin and started our new life with Christ. The old must go before the new can come. According to the Bible, we died to seven things when we were baptized:

First, we died to God's Law because it could not make us right with God:

> In the same way, my friends, **you have died to the law** through the body of Christ. (Ro.7:4 NRSV; Ga.2:19)

Second, we died to the basic principles of this world because we could not stop sinning on our own. The basic principles of this world say that if one is commanded to do something, he is expected to do it by himself:

> **Since you died with Christ to the basic principles of this world** . . . (Co.2:20 NIV)

Third, we died to the power of sin; for it was stronger than we were. The power of sin forced us to disobey God by making us choose:

> Shall we continue in sin. . ? Certainly not! **How shall we who died to sin live any longer in it?** (Ro.6:2 NKJV)

Fourth, we died to our sinful nature because we could not stop our sinful desires:

> *Those who belong to Christ Jesus* **have crucified the sinful nature** *with its passions and desires.* (Ga.5:24 NIV; Co.2:11)

Fifth, we died to our old self because we were selfish. We were addicted to pleasing ourselves:

> *We know that* **our old self was crucified with him** *so that the body of sin might be destroyed.* (Ro 6:6 NRSV; Eph 4:22; Co.3:9)

Sixth, we died to the world (Satan's kingdom) because Satan controlled us:

> *May I never boast of anything except the cross of our Lord Jesus Christ,* **by which the world has been crucified to me,** *and* **I to the world.** (Ga.6:14 NRSV)

Seventh, we died to ourselves because we were the problem. Christians no longer run their own lives because they have given Christ control. Now He is our master. Jesus Christ controls every part of our lives:

> **I have been crucified with Christ**; *it is no longer I who live, but* **Christ lives in me**. (Ga.2:20 NKJV; Co.3:3)

We died to these seven things when we were baptized. The word *baptism* means "to go under water." When someone is baptized, he goes under water into Christ's death. At times, Satan tells me that I did not die to the power of sin. At those times, I remember the following Bible verses:

> **We died to sin; how can we live in it any longer?** *Or don't you know that all of us who* **were baptized into Christ Jesus were baptized into his death?** *We* **were therefore buried with him through baptism into death** *in order that, just as Christ was raised from the dead through the glory of the Father,* **we too may live a new life.** (Ro.6:2-4 NIV)

In our baptism, we died to the power of sin. We no longer need to overcome the power of sin because Christ overcame it. When we were baptized, we also died to the sinful nature with its desire for evil:

> *In him you were also circumcised,* **in the putting off of <u>the sinful nature</u>,** *... having been buried with him* <u>**in baptism**</u> *and raised with him through your faith in the power of God,* (Co.2:11-12 NIV)

We no longer need to overcome our sinful nature. For by the Holy Spirit living in our lives, we now have His divine nature. The Bible says that we died to sin and our sinful nature in our baptism. Therefore, we do not stop our sins by our own efforts. Rather, we believe that we died to the power of sin in our baptism and that the Holy Spirit lives in us:

> So you also **must consider yourselves dead to sin** and alive to God in Christ Jesus. (Ro.6:11 NRSV)

The Bible is truth. We must no longer say, act, or think that our sinful nature or the power of sin is alive in us:

> But put on the Lord Jesus Christ, and **make no provision for the flesh**, to fulfill its lusts. (Ro.13:14 NKJV)

Through our baptism, we died to the seven things that caused us to sin. Therefore, a person must be baptized before he starts his new life with Christ:

> Therefore, **_if_ anyone is in Christ**, he **is a new creation; old things have passed away**; behold, all things have become new. (1Co.5:17 NKJV)

THE NEW LIFE WITH CHRIST

When we died in our baptism, the Holy Spirit began to live in us. From that time on, Christ has controlled our lives:

> **For you died**, and your life is hidden with Christ **in God**. When **Christ _who is_ our life** appears, then you also will appear with Him in glory. (Co.3:3-4 NKJV)

We do not stop sinning merely because of our death. Rather, we overcome our sins because Christ lives in us, controlling us. We must believe that Christ controls our lives:

> Likewise you also, **reckon yourselves** to be dead indeed to sin, but **alive to God in Christ Jesus our Lord.** (Ro.6:11 NKJV)

Christ entered us when we were baptized:

> For **all of you who were baptized into Christ have clothed yourselves with Christ**. (Ga.3:27 NASB)

Christ's Holy Spirit lives in us. He changes our actions from the inside of us. The Holy Spirit replaced the seven things that made us sin. The Holy Spirit controls us so that we please God. Therefore, we no longer need to know God's Law, for the Holy Spirit reveals to us God's will:

> But now, by dying to what once bound us, **we have been released from the law** so that **we serve in the new way of the Spirit**. (Ro.7:6.NIV)

The Holy Spirit stops our sinful actions. Therefore, we no longer try to stop our sins by our own strength. Rather, we trust in the Holy Spirit:

> If **_by the Spirit you are putting to death_** the deeds of the body, you will live (Ro.8:13 NASB)

The Holy Spirit is stronger than the power of sin. Since the Holy Spirit lives in us, we are no longer pushed around by the power of sin:

> I pray that out of his glorious riches **he may strengthen you <u>with power through his Spirit</u> in your inner being.** (Eph.3:16-17 NIV)

The Holy Spirit gave us God's divine nature. Therefore, we do not want to sin; for God's holy nature replaced our sinful nature:

> **Through them you** may escape from the corruption that is in the world because of lust, and **may become participants <u>of the divine nature</u>**. (2Pe 1:4 NRSV)

The Holy Spirit changes our minds so that we now live to please God. We are no longer self-centered but our focus is to be like God in our attitudes, behavior, and character:

> You **were taught** to put away **your former way of life**, **your old self, corrupt** and deluded by its lusts, and **to be renewed in the spirit** of your minds, and to **clothe yourselves with the new self, created according <u>to the likeness of God in true righteousness and holiness</u>**. (Eph.4:22-24 NRSV)

The Holy Spirit protects us from Satan because we are God's children. In other words, Satan can no longer bully us:

> We know that **those who are born of God** do not sin, but **<u>the one who was born of God protects them</u>**, and **the evil one does not touch them**. (1Jn.5:18 NRSV)

Finally, the Holy Spirit controls our lives because we gave our lives to Christ in our baptism. Now, the Holy Spirit causes us to act like Christ:

> **May the God** of peace . . . **equip you** with everything good **for doing his will**, and **may he work in us** what is pleasing to him, through Jesus Christ, to whom be glory for ever and ever. Amen. (He.13:20-21 NIV)

Since God controls our lives, He causes us to live for Him. We no longer try to change ourselves. Rather, we always ask God to change us:

> Work out your salvation with fear and trembling; for **it is God who is at work in you**, both **to will and to work for His good pleasure**. (Php.3:12-13 NASB)

Satan still tempts us. But God controls the ways that Satan can tempt us:

> *No temptation has seized you except* what is common to man. And *God is faithful; he will not let you be tempted beyond what you can bear.* But when you are tempted, *he will also provide a way out so that you can stand up under it.* (1Co.10:13 NIV)

When Satan tempts us, God promises to give us strength. For this reason, we obey and trust God:

> *May the God of peace* himself *sanctify you entirely;* and may *your <u>spirit</u> and <u>soul</u> and <u>body</u> be kept* sound and blameless at the coming of our Lord Jesus Christ. *The one who calls you is faithful, and he will do this.* (1Th.5:23-24 NRSV)

God will keep us strong to the end:

> You are not lacking in any spiritual gift as you wait for the revealing of our Lord Jesus Christ. *He will also strengthen you to the end,* so that you may be blameless on the day of our Lord Jesus Christ. (1Co.1:7-8 NRSV)

Our baptism would only be a bath of ritual if the Holy Spirit did not enter us. We are not saved if we simply went under water. Rather, we are saved if we have given our lives to God through our baptism. Then, the Holy Spirit lives in us:

> *He saved us* through the *washing of rebirth <u>and</u> the renewal by the Holy Spirit.* (Ti.3:5 NIV)

The Holy Spirit is the Spirit of God and Jesus Christ. Since the Holy Spirit lives in us, God and Jesus Christ also live in us:

> For in Christ *all the fullness of the Deity* lives in bodily form, and *you have been given fullness in Christ.* (Co.2:9-10 NIV)

We will overcome our sins because the fullness of Jesus Christ controls us:

> The mind of sinful man is death, but *the mind controlled by the Spirit is life* and peace. (Ro.8:6 NIV)

Because of Jesus Christ, we are new people. Therefore, Christians are people who are controlled by God:

> Therefore, if anyone *is in Christ,* he *is a new creation;* the *old has gone,* the *new has come!* (1Co.5:17 NIV)

CHRIST CLEANS OUR HEARTS

Normally, people are baptized in water; and then they receive the

Holy Spirit (Ac.2). However, God does not always follow this order. Sometimes, a person is baptized in water, and then he receives the Holy Spirit at a later time (Ac.8:1-7). Other times, a person receives the Holy Spirit and then is baptized later with water (Ac.10:24-48). There is no specific order. However, people who believe in Jesus must be baptized; and they must receive the Holy Spirit. Before we received the Holy Spirit, God cleaned our hearts:

> Neither is **new wine** put **into old wineskins**; otherwise, the skins burst, and the wine is spilled, and the skins are destroyed; but **new wine is put into fresh wineskins, and so both are preserved."** (Mt 9:17 NRSV)

The new wine is the Holy Spirit. The old wine skin is man's wicked heart. We had wicked hearts when we were born into this world:

> **The heart is deceitful above all things, and desperately wicked:** who can know it? (Jer.17:9 KJV)

When we were baptized, the Holy Spirit actually came into our hearts:

> Because you are sons, God has **sent forth the Spirit of His Son <u>into our hearts</u>**, crying, "Abba! Father!" (Ga.4:6 NASB; 2Co.1:22)

God is holy. He cannot put up with sin (wickedness). Hence, His Holy Spirit cannot live in a wicked heart. Before Jesus died, God promised to give new hearts to His people. God also promised to put His Spirit in our new hearts:

> I will sprinkle clean water on you, and you will be clean; I will cleanse you from all your impurities and from all your idols. **I will give you a new heart and put a new spirit in you**; **I will remove from you your heart of stone and give you a heart of flesh**. And **I will put my Spirit in you and move you to follow my decrees and be careful to keep my laws**.
> (Eze.36:25-27 NIV)

The Bible refers to baptism as "the washing of rebirth":

> Christ saved us, not because of righteous things we had done, but because of His mercy. He saved us through **the washing of rebirth** and **renewal by the Holy Spirit**." (Ti.3:5 NIV)

Through our baptism, God removed our sins and cleaned our hearts:

> And now why are you waiting? Arise and **be baptized, and <u>wash away your sins</u>**, calling on the name of the Lord.' (Ac.22:16 NKJV)

Remember that if someone truly believes in Jesus, he will be baptized. God cleaned the sin from our hearts when we by faith are believed. At that time, God also gave us His Holy Spirit:

> "So **God, who knows the heart**, acknowledged them by **giving them the Holy Spirit,** just as He did to us, and made no distinction between us and them, **purifying their hearts by faith.** (Ac.15:9 NKJV)

God knows our hearts. According to God, Christians have pure hearts. A person will not see God if he does not have a pure (clean) heart:

> Blessed are **the pure in heart, for they shall see God.** (Mt.5:8 NASB)

God hears a Christian's prayers because he has a pure heart:

> Flee from youthful lusts and pursue righteousness, faith, love and peace, **with those who call on the Lord from a pure heart.** (2Ti.2:22 NASB)

Because we obeyed God's covenant, the Holy Spirit came into our hearts. Once the Holy Spirit controls our hearts, we think good thoughts and act in good ways:

> The good man **brings good things out of the good stored up in his heart**, and the evil man brings evil things **out of the evil stored up in his heart**. For **out of the overflow of his heart his mouth speaks**.
> (Lk.6:45 NIV)

Because we believed in Jesus, we turned to God and were baptized. At that time, we gave God control of our lives. Therefore, God forgave our sins and gave us the Holy Spirit. The Holy Spirit changes us to become like Christ.

For Further Thought:

I am afraid to give God control of my life because...

1. Why must we obey God's covenant?

2. What is repentance?

3. Why does belief always cause a change in action?

4. What seven things died in our water baptism?

5. What is the difference between the old (that is gone) and the new (that has come)?

6. What happens when we give Christ control of our lives?

7. How do we get a pure heart?

8. According to the Bible, how do we call on the name of the Lord Jesus?

Memory Verse:
Therefore, if anyone is in Christ, he is a new creation; the old has gone, the new has come!   1 Corinthians 5:17

Notes:

Step 4

Assessing the Damage

STEP 4 *We will assess our attitudes, behavior, and character by the Scripture, asking God's Spirit to reveal any sin in us.*

CAN EVIL MEN SET STANDARDS?

Did you give complete control of your life to Jesus Christ? If you did **not**, the following steps will not help you. They cannot help you until you make Jesus your master (Lord). Once Christ is your Lord, your next step is to make an inventory (list) of your sinful actions. However, who decides whether an action is right or wrong? According to society, what most people think decides what is right or wrong, but people are always changing their ideas according to what they want to do. They do not keep a constant standard:

> *When they measure themselves by themselves and compare themselves with themselves, they are not wise.* (2Co.10:12 NIV)

Over time, people lower their standards. They begin to think what was wrong at one time is no longer wrong. Therefore, their standards of right and wrong change. Sinful people cannot decide the standard of right and wrong because they are easily misled:

> ***Evil men and impostors*** *will grow worse and worse,* ***deceiving and being deceived****.* (2Ti.3:13 NKJV)

People judge an action by its end result. They think that to do right for the wrong reason or do wrong for the right reason makes the action good. Both are wrong according to God:

> ***There is a way which seems right to a man****, but its end is the way of death.* (Pr.14:12 NASB)

All people were born with sinful natures which affect their thinking. Therefore, they cannot make the standard for right and wrong actions.

CAN THE CHURCH SET STANDARDS?

Some people think that the church should set the standard. However, even the church has changed over time. When I was a child, the church's standard was totally different than it is today. God and His Bible have not changed, but the church has taken on the world's values. God warned us that the church would turn away from His truth:

> *For a time is coming when people **will no longer listen to sound and wholesome teaching**. They will follow their own desires and will look for teachers **who will tell them whatever their itching ears want to hear**. **They will reject the truth and chase after myths**.* (2Ti.4:3-4 NLT)

In the church, false teachers mix the world's lies with God's truth. They corrupt God's truth:

> *But false prophets also arose among the people, just as **there will also be false teachers among you**, who will **secretly introduce destructive heresies**, even denying the Master who bought them, bringing swift destruction upon themselves.* (2Pe.2:1 NASB; Ac.20:30-31; Ga.2:4)

False teachers say that God loves people and that He will ignore their sin. These teachers twist God's truth so that Christians think that they can sin and still go to heaven:

> *For certain men whose condemnation was written about long ago **have secretly slipped in among you**. They are godless men, **who change the grace of our God into a license for immorality** and deny Jesus Christ our only Sovereign and Lord.* (Jude 1:4 NIV)

Do not suppose that people are Christians when they say, "I love Jesus." Instead, the true way to tell if a person is a Christian is if they begin to act like Jesus and obey God:

> ***Not everyone who says to me, 'Lord, Lord,' will enter the kingdom of heaven, but only the one who does the will of my Father in heaven***. *On that day many will say to me, "Lord, Lord, did we not prophesy in your name, and cast out demons in your name, and do many deeds of power in your name?" Then I will declare to them, **"I never knew you; go away from me, you evildoers**.*" (Mt.7:21-23 NRSV)

Do not think that every pastor or teacher in the church is a Christian:

> *For such men **are false apostles, deceitful workers, disguising themselves as apostles of Christ**. Therefore it is not surprising if **his*

servants also disguise themselves as servants of righteousness, whose end will be according to their deeds. (2Co.11:13-14 NASB)

Since Satan has placed his followers in the church, we cannot blindly believe what all people tell us in all churches. Therefore, we cannot even trust the church to set the standard of right and wrong.

OUR CONSCIENCES

God is perfect (sinless). Since God cannot do wrong, He alone can set what is right or wrong:

He is the Rock; **his deeds are perfect. Everything he does is just** and fair. He is a faithful God **who does no wrong**; how just and upright he is! (De 32:4 NLT)

People change their standards, but God does not change. Therefore, God's standard of right and wrong remains the same:

Jesus Christ **is the same yesterday, today, and forever.** (He.13:8 NKJV)

Only God must decide whether our actions are right or wrong. He knows our thoughts and actions. Therefore, He can judge our actions because He knows why we do what we do:

O LORD, **you have searched me and you know me.** You know when I sit and when I rise; **you perceive my thoughts** from afar. You discern my going out and my lying down; **you are familiar with all my ways. Before a word is on my tongue you know it completely**, O LORD. (Ps 139:3-4 NIV)

Since God is both perfect and knows us very well, we must ask Him to show us our sins:

Search me, O God, and know my heart; Try me, and know my anxieties; And **see if there is any wicked way in me**, And lead me in the way everlasting. (Ps.139:23-24 NKJV)

Everyone has a conscience. God uses our consciences to tell us when we have sinned. The Holy Spirit told Paul's conscience when he sinned:

My conscience is clear, but that doesn't prove I'm right. It is the Lord himself who will examine me and decide. (1Co 4:4 NLT)

The Holy Spirit also speaks to our consciences:

We can say with confidence and **a clear conscience** that we have lived with a God-given holiness and sincerity in all our dealings. (2Co.1:12 NLT)

As Christians, we do not judge ourselves; rather, we listen to God's Holy Spirit. Through our consciences, the Holy Spirit tells us when we sin. When we have sinned, we admit our sins to God. We ask God to forgive us and to help us not to sin. Christians aim to have a clear conscience that does not feel any guilt:

> They must hold fast to the mystery of the faith **with a clear conscience**.
> (1Ti 3:9 NIV)

All Christians live by their consciences. The Bible commands us to keep our consciences free from guilt:

> **Keep your conscience clear,** so that, when you are maligned, those who abuse you for your good conduct in Christ may be put to shame.
> (1Pe.3:16 NRSV; He.13:18)

The Holy Spirit speaks through our consciences, judging our thoughts and actions. Therefore, we must ask God to help us make an honest list of our sinful actions. We cannot ask God for help to overcome a sin until we know our sins.

God's Absolute Standard

Thoughts come to our minds. But are they from us, from God, or from Satan? We must find out where our thoughts come from:

> Beloved, do not believe every spirit, **but test the spirits to see whether they are from God**, because many false prophets have gone out into the world.
> (1Jn.4:1 NASB)

Satan sometimes pretends to be the Holy Spirit and plays with our minds. Often, he accuses us of sin when we do not sin and gives us peace when we do sin. He tries to confuse us:

> **No wonder, for even Satan disguises himself as an angel of light**.
> (2Co.11:14 NASB)

Unlike Satan, the Holy Spirit's voice will always agree with the Bible. For the Holy Spirit wrote the Bible, and God does not change:

> God is not a human being, that he should lie, or **a mortal, that he should change his mind.** Has he promised, and will he not do it? Has he spoken, and will he not fulfill it?
> (Nu 23:19 NRSV)

Since the Holy Spirit does not change, what He says in our hearts will always agree with the Bible. We must study the Bible so that we can separate God's truth from Satan's lies:

> Now the Bereans were of more noble character than the Thessalonians, for they received the message with great eagerness and **examined the Scriptures every day to see if what Paul said was true**. (Ac 17:11 NIV, 1Jn.5:13)

God gave us the Scriptures so that we could know which thoughts come from God:

> For the <u>word of God</u> is alive and active. Sharper than any double-edged sword, it penetrates even to dividing soul and spirit, joints and marrow; <u>**it judges the thoughts and attitudes of the heart.**</u> (He.4:12 NIV)

The Bible is God's standard. We judge our thoughts and actions by the Bible because God gave it to instruct and correct us:

> **All Scripture is given by inspiration of God,** and is profitable for doctrine, for reproof, for correction, for instruction in righteousness, **that the man of God may be complete, thoroughly equipped for every good work.** (2Ti.3:16-17 NKJV; 2Pe.1:20-21)

God spoke His words to His prophets, and they wrote His words down:

> We also constantly give thanks to God for this, that **when you received the word of God that you heard from us**, you accepted it not as a human word **but as what it really is, God's word**, which is also at work in you believers. (1Th.2:13 NRSV)

The prophets knew when God was speaking to them. Therefore, they could separate their thoughts from God's voice. Paul is a good example:

> To the married I give this command—**<u>not I</u> but the Lord**—that the wife should not separate from her husband. . . . To the rest I say—**I and <u>not the Lord</u>**—that if any believer has a wife who is an unbeliever, and she consents to live with him, he should not divorce her. (1Co.7:10, 12 NRSV)

Paul knew when it was his own thoughts or when God spoke to him. The New Testament was written by the authority of Jesus. To reject what the New Testament says is to reject God Himself:

> Finally, brothers, **we instructed you how to live in order to please God**, as in fact you are living. Now we ask you and urge you in the Lord Jesus to do this more and more. For you know **what instructions we gave you <u>by</u>**

> **the authority of the Lord Jesus.** ... Therefore, **he who rejects this instruction does not reject man but God**, who gives you his Holy Spirit.
> (1Th.4:1, 2&8 NIV)

God guides us by both the Holy Spirit and the New Testament. Therefore, the Holy Spirit will speak through our consciences telling us whether our thoughts or actions are sin. However, by comparing our thoughts to the Bible, we can make sure that it is the voice of God Who is speaking:

> Learn the meaning of the saying, **"Do not go beyond what is written."** Then you will not take pride in **one man over and against another**.
> (1Co.4:6 NIV)

UNDERSTANDING SIN

Today, many Christians cannot tell when they sin. Sometimes they do evil, sometimes they do not do the good things that they should do, and sometimes they disobey the Holy Spirit's leading. All this is sin. Clearly, God commands us not to do evil. When a person **commits** evil, he disobeys God. This sin is called a sin of **commission**:

> **All wrongdoing is sin.** (1Jn.5:17 NRSV)

When we do harm to ourselves or do wrong to others, we sin. The following verses list some ways that man disobeys God:

> **The acts of the sinful nature are obvious**: sexual immorality, impurity and debauchery; idolatry and witchcraft; hatred, discord, jealousy, fits of rage, selfish ambition, dissensions, factions, and envy; drunkenness, orgies, and the like. **I warn you, as I did before, that those who live like this will not inherit the kingdom of God.** (Ga.5:19-21 NIV)

Therefore, the sin of commission is to commit evil against ourselves or others. If we learn to listen, the Holy Spirit will speak to us when we do a sin of commission.

God also commands us to do good to others. Hence, we must not **omit** doing good for someone in need. If we refuse to help other people, we commit the sin of **omission**:

> Anyone, then, **who knows the right thing to do and fails to do it, commits sin.** (Ja.4:17 NRSV)

We should do the good that the Holy Spirit shows us. Otherwise, we break Christ's law. The law of Christ says that we must love others:

> **A new commandment** I give to you, **that you love one another.**
> (Jn.13:34 NASB)

Sometimes we know people who need help. If we do not help them, we sin. However, if we help others in need, we obey the law of Christ:

> Bear one another's burdens, and in this way **you will fulfill the law of Christ.** (Ga.6:2 NRSV)

The golden rule can guide us so that we will not do the sin of omission:

> **Do to others whatever you would like them to do to you.** This is the essence of all that is taught in the law and the prophets. (Mt.7:12 NLT)

Therefore, the sin of omission is to omit doing good toward others.

The New Testament was not given to replace the Law. The Holy Spirit replaced the Law. Hence, we must listen to His voice. If we do not wait until the Holy Spirit speaks to us and act without being sure of what He is saying, we commit the **sin of indecision**. Every Christian has the ability to hear the Holy Spirit speaking to him through his own conscience. God tells him what to do. Many Christians do not listen to the Holy Spirit. Since they are not sure of what God wants them to do, they commit the sin of indecision:

> But now, by dying to what once bound us, we have been released from the law so that **we serve in the new way of the Spirit**, and not in the old way of the written code. (Ro.7:6 NIV)

The sin of commission and the sin of omission do not have a list of "do and don't" rules like the Ten Commandments. God's Law does not list every way that we could wrong ourselves or our neighbors. For example, the Bible never mentions drug addiction or pornography. Also, the law of Christ does not list good actions from the greatest to the least of importance. When we know of two good things that need to be done at the same time, we need to decide which one is more important. Therefore, God gave us His Spirit. He warns us when we are about to commit evil and reveals to us God's will so that we do not omit doing good:

> "For this is the covenant that I will make with the house of Israel after those days, says the LORD: **I will put My laws in their mind and write them on their hearts**; and I will be their God, and they shall be My people. None of them shall teach his neighbor, and none his brother, saying, 'Know the

> LORD,' **for all shall know Me, from the least of them to the greatest of them."** (He.8:10-11 NKJV)

God's laws are His will for our lives. The Holy Spirit writes God's will on our hearts and minds, moment by moment. We can know God's will because we listen to the Holy Spirit's voice. He warns us before we do wrong. He also tells us the good that God wants us to do. God planned only one good thing for us to do at one time:

> For we are God's workmanship, **created in Christ Jesus to do good works**, which **God prepared in advance for us to do.** (Eph 2:10 NIV)

We should not consider what is the best thing to do, but we should consider what is God's will for us. For we know that His will is the best in all situations. Before we do something, we must listen to the Holy Spirit's voice to hear what He says and to act in faith:

> **Trust in the LORD with all your heart**, and lean not on your own understanding; **in all your ways acknowledge Him**, and **He shall direct your paths.** (Pr.3:5-6 NKJV)

God promises that the Holy Spirit will speak to our hearts. We must listen for His voice in every situation. Otherwise, we will sin because we acted without knowing God's will:

> If we live by the Spirit, **let us also be guided by the Spirit.** (Ga.5:25 NRSV)

We commit the sin of indecision when we make choices without being sure of God's will. Therefore, Christians live by faith that the Holy Spirit is speaking to them:

> **Whatever is not from faith is sin.** (Ro.14:23 NASB)

THE THREE AREAS OF SIN

According to the Bible, a person can sin in his actions, thoughts, or attitudes. These three areas are listed in 1 John:

> For all that is in the world—the **lust of the flesh**, the **lust of the eyes**, and **the pride of life**—is not of the Father but is of the world. (1Jn.2:16-17 NKJV)

When we sin with our bodies, we do things that are sinful. When we sin with our eyes, we sin through our soul by thinking sinful thoughts. When we sin by our pride, we sin through our spirits. We take the credit for what God has done or has given us.

The first area of sin is with our actions. When Jesus became our Lord, He first dealt with our sinful actions. Jesus asked:

> **Why do you call Me, 'Lord,** Lord,**' and do not do what I say**?
> (Lk.6:46 NASB)

Some churchgoers live to appease God. They live up to their churches' standards. But Christians live to please God. They listen for the Holy Spirit and study the Bible:

> Do not be deceived: God cannot be mocked. A man reaps what he sows. The one who sows to **please his sinful nature,** from that nature **will reap destruction**; the one who **sows to please the Spirit**, from the Spirit **will reap eternal life.**
> (Ga.6:7-8 NIV)

God requires that our sinful actions stop. The Holy Spirit shows us our sins and then puts them to death so that we no longer do those things:

> Therefore, dear brothers and sisters, you have no obligation to do what your sinful nature urges you to do. For if you live by its dictates, **you will die.** But if through the power of the Spirit **you put to death the deeds of your sinful nature, you will live.** For all who are led by the Spirit of God are children of God.
> (Ro.8:13-14 NLT)

Our sinful actions stop because the Holy Spirit controls us. He gives us the strength to say "No!" Therefore, we take an inventory of our sinful actions so that we can seek God's help to change our behavior.

The second area of sin is in our thoughts. The lust of the eyes are sins that we do in our thoughts:

> **All of us used to live that way, <u>following the passionate desires and inclinations</u> of our sinful nature.** By our very nature we were subject to God's anger, just like everyone else.
> (Eph.2:3 NLT)

Many people do not do sinful actions because others might find out. Yet they continue to think sinful thoughts. According to God, sinful thoughts and sinful actions are equally wrong:

> But I say to you that **everyone who looks at a woman with lust** has **already committed adultery with her** in his heart.
> (Mt.5:28 NRSV)

When you watch a sinful movie, you passively take part in its sin by what you are thinking. Some people enjoy sin in their thoughts. But God will judge their thoughts as if they actually did what they were thinking:

> God will judge **the secrets of men** through Christ Jesus.
> (Ro.2:16 NASB; He.4:12)

Christ died to stop our sinful thoughts:

> Just think how much more **the blood of Christ** will **purify our consciences from sinful deeds** so that we can worship the living God.
> (He.9:14 NLT)

Since the Holy Spirit controls our minds, He will put to death our sinful thoughts. Also, He will focus our thoughts on God's will:

> Those who live according to **the sinful nature have their minds set on what that nature desires**; but those who live in accordance with **the Spirit have their minds set on what the Spirit desires.** (Ro.8:5 NIV)

Therefore, we must take an inventory of our thoughts. Our sinful thoughts offend God just as much as our sinful actions.

The third area of sin is our motives (reasons for doing the action) and attitudes (the emotion while doing the action). People sin when they do good things for the wrong reasons. For example, some people give money to charities so that they can pay less taxes. Their actions are good, but their reasons are wrong. The reason for an action is just as important as the action:

> Therefore do not go on passing judgment before the time, but wait until the Lord comes **who will both bring to light the things hidden in the darkness** and **disclose the motives of men's hearts.** (1Co 4:5 NASB)

God will judge our actions and our motives. Other people do good but become angry while doing it because they have many other things to do. God will also judge the attitude in which we do the good works:

> **For the word of God is living and powerful**, and sharper than any two-edged sword, piercing even to the division of soul and spirit, and of joints and marrow, and **is a discerner of the thoughts and intents of the heart.**
> (He.4:12 NKJV)

Hate is a very strong feeling, and God hates sinful attitudes:

> There are six things that **the LORD hates**, seven that are an abomination to him: **haughty eyes**, a lying tongue, and hands that shed innocent blood,

> *a **heart that devises wicked plans**, feet **that hurry to run to evil**, a lying witness who testifies falsely, and **one who sows discord in a family**.*
> (Pro.6:16-19 NRSV)

Most Christians think that murder and sexual sin are worse than sinful attitudes. But sinful attitudes bother God as much as sinful actions. God hates pride:

> *"The fear of the LORD **is to hate evil; pride and arrogance** and the evil way and the perverted mouth, I hate.* (Pr.8:13 NASB)

Pride is sin because it takes God's credit from Him. Prideful people think that they made themselves who they are. They only fool themselves:

> *For if anyone **thinks himself to be something**, when he is nothing, **he deceives himself**.* (Ga.6:3 NKJV)

God gives people everything that they have. God makes Christians who they are:

> *For **who makes you different from anyone else**? What do you have **that you did not receive**? And if you did receive it, **why do you boast as though you did not**?* (1Co 4:7 NIV)

The Holy Spirit lives in Christians. He changes us so that we act like Christ. We must always be sure to thank God for all that He has done in us:

> *I am the vine, you are the branches; he who abides in Me and I in him, he bears much fruit, for **apart from Me you can do nothing**.*
> (Jn.15:5 NASB)

A prideful attitude is the opposite of a humble attitude. We become humble when we realize that we are nothing without God, for it is God who helps us. God will continue to help us if we are humble:

> *And all of you, serve each other in humility, for "**God opposes the proud but favors the humble**." So **humble yourselves** under the mighty power of God, and at the right time he will lift you up in honor.*
> (1Pe.5:5-7 NLT)

If we become proud, God will no longer help us. In the past, many famous preachers thought that they were great Christians. So God removed His grace, leaving them to stand by their own strength. Without God's help, they became trapped in sin. God showed them that they could not be holy without Him. We must realize that we are weak by ourselves. Then, we can ask God and receive His help (grace):

> He said to me, "**My grace** is sufficient for you, **for power is made perfect in weakness.**" So, **I will boast all the more gladly of my weaknesses**, so that the power of Christ may dwell in me. (2Co.12:9 NRSV)

Paul took no credit for his success. Instead, he praised God for what He had helped him become:

> But **by the grace of God I am what I am**, and his grace to me was not without effect. No, I worked harder than all of them **yet not I, but the grace of God** that was with me. (1Co.15:10 NIV)

All Christians must readily say that the Holy Spirit is the One Who changes their lives:

> **It is because of him that you are in Christ Jesus**, who has become for us wisdom from God—that is, **our righteousness, holiness and redemption.** Therefore, as it is written: "Let him who boasts **boast in the Lord."** (1Co.1:30-31 NLT)

There are many attitudes which are sinful, but God hates pride the most. We must ask the Holy Spirit to show us our sinful character. In conclusion, we must take an inventory of our sinful actions, thoughts, and attitudes. Then, we can boldly come to God and humbly ask Him for the help we need:

> Let us therefore **come boldly to the throne of grace**, that we may **obtain mercy** and **find grace to help in time of need.** (He.4:16 NKJV)

For Further Thought:

The areas of my life that I protect myself by denial are...

1. Why can't people set the standard of right and wrong?

2. How do we overcome self-deception while doing a moral inventory?

3. Why can only God set the standard of right and wrong?

4. Describe the three types of sin.

5. Why can only Christians commit the sin of indecision?

6. Why do we deal first with the acts of the sinful nature?

7. Why must we take an inventory of our thoughts?

8. Why must Christians deal with their pride and other attitudes?

Memory Verse:
Examine yourselves to see whether you are in the faith; test yourselves. Do you not realize that Christ Jesus is in you— unless, of course, you fail the test?   2Corinthians 13:5

NOTES:

Step 5

Facing the Facts

Step 5 *We will be honest with ourselves, confess our sins to God, and specifically admit to a mature Christian the sins of our past.*

All Have Sinned

In step 4, we took an inventory of our sinful actions. Because many people fear what others will think about their sins, they deny their ongoing sins. However, all people are born prone to sins that they cannot stop on their own:

> *Indeed, there **is not a righteous man on earth who continually does good and who never sins.*** (Ec.7:20 NASB)

Your sins are not worse than other people's sins, for God considers all sins to be equally wrong. He will judge the liars just like He will judge the sexually immoral:

> *For whoever keeps the whole law and **yet stumbles at just one point is guilty of breaking all of it**. For he who said, "Do not commit adultery," also said, "Do not murder." If you do not commit adultery but do commit murder, **you have become a law-breaker**.* (Ja.2:10-11 NIV)

Normally, we want to hide our sins because we do not want others to see our weaknesses. However, we need to start by being honest with ourselves in step 5.

Confronting Our Sin

The New Testament states that there are three different ways to respond to our sin. I call them the three "if's." Some people think that they are good people. They excuse their sins as normal behavior; they know that no one is perfect. However, these people lie to themselves. They respond to sin with the **first "if"**:

> *If we say that we have no sin, we are deceiving ourselves* and the truth is not in us.　　　　　　　　　　　　　　　　　(1Jn.1:8 NASB)

When I was a teenager, the world taught us that alcoholics are sick, that homosexuals are sexually disoriented, and that the sexually immoral are liberated. They denied that God is real, thinking that their denial allowed them to judge what morally acceptable behavior is. God said:

> Do not deceive yourselves. *If you think that you are wise in this age,* you should become fools so that you may become wise. For **the wisdom of this world is foolishness with God.**　　　(1Co.3:18-19 NRSV)

Many people have denied the concept of sin; they deny that they have disobeyed God. They deny the idea of moral absolutes--that some things will always be wrong. People think that doing bad for the right reasons or doing good for the wrong reasons is okay. This kind of thinking is morally relative. These people are always trying to find good in everything and in everyone. They see themselves as good people who have made some poor choices. They think that they are good because they only reflect on the good they have done. Nevertheless, we have all sinned. All the good that we have done cannot cancel out one of our sins:

> For **all of us have become like one who is unclean,** And **all our righteous deeds** are like a filthy garment.　　　(Isa.64:6 NASB)

To focus on the good that we have done while ignoring the sin in our own lives is foolish. Have you ever lied? Have you ever taken something that was not yours? Guys, have you ever looked at a woman with lust? Girls, have you ever wanted what someone else had? One sin, any sin, makes you imperfect. God cannot let imperfect people into heaven; otherwise, heaven would be no better than life on earth. Admit that you have sinned, that you have broken God's Law. To continue to deny that you have sinned will not save you from hell:

> *Do not be deceived: God cannot be mocked.* A man reaps what he sows. **The one who sows to please his sinful nature, from that nature will reap destruction**; the one who sows to please the Spirit, from the Spirit will reap eternal life.　　　　　　　　　　　(Ga.6:7-8 NIV)

Since God created the universe, we must come to terms that only He has the right to make the rules. We must not deny the idea of sin. We must believe in God and deal with our sins through Jesus Christ.

TAKING RESPONSIBILITY

Christians must respond to sin with the **second "if."** They must agree with God and admit their sinful actions to Him. Then, He will forgive their sins and remove the sins from their lives:

> *If we confess our sins*, **He is** faithful and just **to forgive us our sins** and **to cleanse us from all unrighteousness.** (1Jn.1:9 NKJV)

Some people admit that they have sinned, but they refuse to admit that they are the problem. These people blame others for their sins. They are just like Adam and Eve who refused to be responsible for their sins. Adam blamed Eve; and Eve blamed the snake:

> "Who told you that you were naked?" the LORD God asked. "Have you eaten from the tree whose fruit I commanded you not to eat?" The man replied, **"It was the woman you gave me who gave me the fruit,** and I ate it." Then the LORD God asked the woman, "What have you done?" **The serpent deceived me,"** she replied. **"That's why I ate it."** (Ge.3:11-13NLT)

When we blame others, we do not take away our guilt before God. We must be like Paul. He knew that he was responsible for his sins:

> **Even though I was formerly a blasphemer, a persecutor, and a man of violence.** But I received mercy because I had acted ignorantly in unbelief, and the grace of our Lord overflowed for me with the faith and love that are in Christ Jesus. The saying is sure and worthy of full acceptance, that **Christ Jesus came into the world to save sinners—<u>of whom I am</u> the foremost.** (1Ti.1:13-15 NRSV)

No person forced us to sin, and we must not blame others for our sins. Rather, we must confess our sins one by one. We must agree with God that we have sinned against Him. We must admit that we alone are responsible for our actions:

> Wash away all my iniquity and cleanse me from my sin. **For I know my transgressions, and my sin is always before me.** Against you, you only, **have I sinned** and done what is evil in your sight, so that you are proved right when you speak and justified when you judge. (Ps.51:2-4 NIV)

We must first admit to ourselves that we have sinned. Otherwise, we will never admit our sins to God or another Christian. Therefore, let us admit that we ourselves are responsible for our sin. Then, God will forgive our sins and remove them from our lives (1Jn.1:9).

SIN WILL ALWAYS BE SIN

Many churchgoers believe that some actions are no longer sin. These people do the **third "if"**:

> **_If_ we say that we have not sinned,** we make Him a liar and His word is not in us. (1Jn.1:10 NASB)

Today, we live in the age of information. While the church has gained much knowledge, it does not know the Bible. The Scriptures warn us:

> **. . . always learning and never able to come to the knowledge of the truth.** (2Ti 3:7 NKJV)

"If you want to live together, I recommend that church." If you want to be a drunkard, I recommend this church." A person looks for a church that says his sins are no longer sin:

> For the time is coming **when people will not put up with sound doctrine**, but having itching ears, **they will accumulate for themselves teachers to suit their own desires**, and will turn away from listening to the truth and wander away to myths. (2Ti.4:3-4 NLT)

Today, churches vote about whether certain actions are sins. An excellent example is divorce and remarriage. Fifty years ago, I did not know of any Christians who were remarried. Remarriage of a divorced person was considered a sin. However, many churches have voted on whether remarriage is still a sin. The majority overruled the Bible:

> I urge you, brothers, to watch out for those who cause divisions and **put obstacles in your way that are contrary to the teaching you have learned.**. (Ro.16:17 NIV)

If the Bible calls an action sinful, that action will be a sin forever. God will judge us according to the Bible. Christians do not get to decide whether the Bible is right; rather, the Bible judges whether our decisions or actions are right. For we have been warned:

> *See to it that no one **takes you captive through hollow and deceptive philosophy**, which depends **on human tradition** and the basic **principles of this world** rather than on Christ.* (Co.2:8 NIV)

Many teachers tell you not to worry about your sin because God loves you. These preachers are sincere, but do not be fooled by their sincerity:

> *I am telling you this **so no one will deceive you with well-crafted arguments**.* (Co.2:4 NLT; Co.2:8)

Even though the church has decided that many actions are no longer sin, God has not changed. Therefore, we must ignore the lies from the church. We must read the Bible and confess those actions that the Bible tells us are sin:

> *Anyone who **runs ahead and does not continue in the teaching of Christ** does not have God.* (2Jo 1:9 NIV)

CONFESSING SIN TO GOD

When we sin, we are rebelling against God. We must confess our sins to God when His Holy Spirit points them out in our lives:

> *For I acknowledge my transgressions, and **my sin is always before me. Against You, You only, have I sinned,** and **done this evil in Your sight**—that You may be found just when You speak, and blameless when You judge.* (Ps.51:3-4 NKJV)

When we confess our sins to God, we must admit the specific acts of sin. God knows everything that we have done. But we must still confess our sins to God personally, apologizing to Him for our actions:

> ***When I kept silent about my sin**, my body wasted away Through my groaning all day long. For day and night Your hand was heavy upon me; My vitality was drained away as with the fever heat of summer. Selah. **I acknowledged my sin to You, And my iniquity I did not hide**; I said, "I will confess my transgressions to the LORD"; And **You forgave the guilt of my sin.** Selah.* (Ps.32:3-5 NASB)

We must humbly come to God with our sin:

> ***If we confess our sins,** He is faithful and just **to forgive us our sins** and **to cleanse us from all unrighteousness**.* (1Jn.1:9 NKJV)

Once we confess our sins, God promises to do two things. First, He gives us His mercy. Mercy can only be given after we have sinned. Through His mercy, God forgives our sins:

> People who conceal their sins will not prosper, but **if they confess and turn from them, they will receive mercy.** (Pr.28:13 NLT)

Second, God gives us His grace. Grace can only be given before we sin again. It gives us the strength to say "no" to sin before we do it. Through His grace, we can stop our sins:

> For the grace of God that brings salvation has appeared to all men. It teaches us **to say "No" to ungodliness and worldly passions**, and **to live self-controlled, upright and godly lives** in this present age.
> (Ti 2:11-12 NIV)

The point is that sooner or later everyone will confess their sins to God. You can confess your sins to God now and receive both mercy and grace, or you can wait until judgment day and receive justice:

> So then **each of us shall give account of himself to God.**
> (Ro.14:12 NKJV; 1Pe 4:5)

If you confess your sins now, God will forgive you and help you to stop your sins. But if you wait until after you are dead, God will give you the full punishment for your sins:

> **If we deliberately keep on sinning** after we have received the knowledge of the truth, no sacrifice for sins is left, but **only a fearful expectation of judgment and of raging fire that will consume the enemies of God.** (He.10:26 NIV)

Therefore, we must confess our sins to God while He is willing to forgive us and help us overcome them. When we confess our sins to God, we admit our specific sins that the Holy Spirit has shown us.

Confessing Sin to Another Person

Finally, we must confess our sins to a mature Christian. There is a fear that Satan places in our hearts that Christians will hate us if they know our past sins. For this reason, we need to silence the fear by telling one mature Christian about our sin. There are three things that happen when we confess our sins to a mature Christian. First, the Christian will forgive and accept us:

> *And be kind to one another, tenderhearted, **forgiving one another, just as God in Christ forgave you**.* (Eph.4:32 NKJV)

All Christians must forgive and accept us if we repent of our sins:

> ***If your brother sins, rebuke him; and if he repents, forgive him**. And if he sins against you seven times a day, and returns to you seven times, saying, 'I repent,' forgive him'.* (Lk.17:3-4 NASB)

The reason why we confess to a **mature** Christian is that he can help us by teaching us God's truths:

> *If another believer is overcome by some sin, **you who are godly should gently and humbly help that person back onto the right path**. And be careful not to fall into the same temptation yourself. **Share each other's burdens**, and in this way obey the law of Christ.* (Ga.6:1-2 NLT)

Second, Christians encourage us and pray for us because they know how we will struggle. All of us have been there. Paul prayed for Christians:

> *To this end also **we pray for you always**, that our God will count you worthy of your calling, and **fulfill every desire for goodness** and the work of faith with power.* (2Th.1:11 NASB)

When we confess our sins to a Christian, he is commanded to pray for us:

> *Therefore **confess your sins to one another**, and **pray for one another**, so that you may be healed.* (Ja.5:16 NRSV)

Third, we encourage others when we give our personal testimony in public. We do not list our sins. Rather, we share the general story of our lives:

> *Also many of those who became believers **confessed and disclosed their practices**.* (Ac.19:18 NRSV)

In our story, we describe our lives before we were Christians. Then, we tell how Jesus has changed us and stopped our sins. Finally, we share what our lives are like with Christ living in us. In our story, we give Jesus the credit for changing our lives. Through our story, we will give people hope that Christ can help them stop their sins. Paul told his story:

> *But God had mercy on me so that Christ **Jesus could use me as a prime example** of his great patience with even the worst sinners. Then others*

will realize that they, too, can believe in him and receive eternal life.
(1Ti.1:16 NLT)

Therefore, we must admit our specific sins to ourselves, to God, and to another Christian in order to experience real forgiveness and acceptance.

SIN OR TEMPTATION

Before we confess our sin, we need to know the difference between a temptation and a sin. Often, Satan accuses us of sin when, in reality, he has placed the temptation (sinful thought) in our minds. Satan does not personally tempt everyone, but he uses his demons to tempt people too. Because Satan controls his demons, he is responsible for all temptations:

> *Do not deprive one another except with consent for a time, that you may give yourselves to fasting and prayer; and come together again **so that Satan does not tempt you** because of your lack of self-control.*
> (1Co 7:5 NKJV)

Everyone faces temptations:

> ***The temptations in your life** are no different from what others experience.*
> (1Co.10:13 NLT)

Temptation is simply Satan presenting us with a choice to disobey God. When Satan tempts us, he tells us how we can disobey God. Christ was tempted just like we are:

> *For we do not have a High Priest who cannot sympathize with our weaknesses, but **was in all points tempted as we are**, yet **without sin**.*
> (He.4:15 NKJV)

Jesus was tempted, but He did not sin. Therefore, we can study the temptations of Jesus to learn the difference between temptation and sin.

In Jesus' **first temptation**, we read:

> *Now when **the tempter** came to Him, he said, "If You are the Son of God, command that these stones become bread.*   (Mt.4:3 NKJV)

In this temptation, Satan gave Jesus a thought to do some act. The thought was for Jesus to make stones into bread. We know that Jesus did not sin in this temptation. The presentation of a thought to do some action was only a temptation and not a sin. At a later time, Jesus made water into wine. Therefore, it was not a sin for Jesus to make stones into bread. However, Jesus was very hungry; for the Holy Spirit had told Him not to eat for 40 days. If Satan could get Jesus to make bread, he would have then tempted Jesus to eat the bread. If Jesus ate the bread, He would have disobeyed God and sinned. Therefore, Satan tempts us to sin by presenting us with choices that will sooner or later cause us to disobey God.

In Jesus' **second temptation**, we read:

> **Then the devil took him** to the holy city and **placed him on the pinnacle of the temple**, saying to him, "If you are the Son of God, throw yourself down." (Mt.4:5-6 NRSV)

In this temptation, Satan took Jesus from the desert to the top of the temple and presented Him with a choice to jump. Before the temptation, God told Jesus to go to the desert. Therefore, Satan took Jesus to a place where Jesus was not supposed to be. Then, Satan told Jesus to jump from the temple to prove that God's angels would catch Him. If Jesus chose to put His life in danger to test God, He would have sinned. Jesus knew that it was wrong to show off God's power for our own glory. The thought and the place were not a sin. Rather, they were part of the temptation. However, if Jesus would have tested God, He would have sinned. Satan gives us thoughts and takes us to places where we could sin. The thought and the place are both part of the temptation. However, they are not sin.

In Jesus' **third temptation** we read:

> Again, **the devil took Him** up on an exceedingly high mountain, and **showed Him all the kingdoms of the world** and their glory. And he said to Him, "All these things I will give You **if You will fall down and worship me**." (Mt.4:8-9 NKJV)

In this temptation, Satan took Jesus to a place—a mountain in Judea. Then, Satan showed Jesus all the kingdoms of the world and presented Jesus with a choice to disobey God. Jesus could not see the whole world from the mountain in Judea. However, He saw the world in His mind. Then, Satan presented Jesus with the following choice: if Jesus worshipped him, Satan would give Jesus all the people in the world. In other words, the temptation was that Jesus would not need to die on a cross to save man from Satan. However, Jesus refused the temptation for two reasons. First, Jesus knew that satanic worship is sin. Satan can place some very evil thoughts in our minds, but remember they are only temptations. Second, Jesus knew that God sent Him to earth to die on a cross to save man from sin and Satan. Temptation can be to do the will of God but in our own way. This also is sin. Therefore, a thought, a place, and a vision can be all part of a temptation. Because of Jesus' example, we know that they are not sin.

Satan tempted Jesus a fourth time. This time, Jesus was telling His disciples about His death. When Jesus stopped speaking, Peter said, "This shall never happen to you!" (Mt.16:22 NIV). Then Jesus said:

> **Get behind Me, Satan!** *You are a stumbling block to Me; for you are not setting your mind on God's interests, but man's."* (Mt 16:23 NASB)

Peter spoke because he loved Jesus. Peter did not want Jesus to die. However, Peter's answer did not come from himself. Rather, it came from Satan who gave Peter the thought of what to say. Through Peter, Satan tempted Jesus to not die on a cross. Jesus knew that Satan had placed the thought in Peter's mind. Therefore, Jesus rebuked Satan instead of Peter. From this temptation, we learn that Satan does not tempt us out loud with words. Rather, he places his temptations directly into our minds in thoughts. Sometimes, Satan fills our minds with many temptations to make us believe that our sinful nature did not die. However, we know that our sinful nature is dead because the Bible says so (Ga.5:24; Co.2:11). When our sinful nature was alive, sinful thoughts came from us. Since our sinful nature is dead, sinful thoughts come from the outside from Satan and his demons. Therefore, do not be concerned when a wicked thought pops into your mind. Satan put it there. We must deal with Satan as Jesus did by telling him to leave.

In all four temptations, Jesus was not guilty of sin. Satan will give us complete thoughts that present us with a choice to disobey God. But we are not guilty of the sins if we do not think on them. Satan will take us to places where we could sin. But we are not guilty of sin if we do not stay there. Satan will place visions in our minds that are evil. But we are not guilty of sin if we refuse to continue to think on them:

> But I say, **anyone who even looks at a woman <u>with lust</u>** has already committed adultery with her in his heart. (Mt.5:28 NLT)

However, if we continue to think on the presentation to sin in the theaters of our minds, we have sinned. Anytime that Satan tempts us with sinful thoughts, we must command Satan to leave us. Jesus showed us how:

> Jesus said to him, **"Away with you, Satan!"** (Mt 4:10 NKJV; Mt 16:23)

When we are tempted, we have the authority to command Satan to leave. In conclusion, thoughts, places, and visions are part of temptation. They are not a sin. Therefore, we do not confess temptations. Rather, we confess our sins to ourselves, to God, and to another Christian.

ACCUSATION OR CONVICTION

Since we must confess our specific sins, we must learn to separate conviction from accusation. When God convicts us, His Spirit shows us that we sinned through a specific action. When Satan accuses us, he blames us for many sins at one time. God gave us the Bible, to help us separate conviction from accusation:

> To the Jews who had believed him, Jesus said, "If you hold to my teaching, you are really my disciples. **Then you will know the truth, and the truth will set you free."** (Jn.8:31-32 NIV)

Through the Bible, we learn the truth about Satan's accusations. Often, Satan places evil thoughts in our minds (temptation). Then he blames us for having the sinful thoughts (accusation). Satan tempts and then accuses. Satan is called the accuser of Christians:

> This great dragon—**the ancient serpent called the devil, or Satan,** the one deceiving the whole world—was thrown down to the earth with all his angels... **For the accuser of our brothers** and sisters has been thrown down to earth—**the one who accuses them before our God** day and night. (Re.12:9-10 NLT)

Sometimes, Satan tempts us many times in a row. Then he accuses us by sounding like the Spirit of God. Satan tells us that we are wicked. He tells us that we are too sinful for heaven. Satan tells us that our sinful nature did not die in our baptism. Satan will do anything to make us give up and sin. He even pretends to be God's servant:

> No wonder, for even **Satan disguises himself as an angel of light**. Therefore it is not surprising **if his servants also disguise themselves as servants of righteousness**, whose end will be according to their deeds. (2Co.11:14 NASB)

When we take an inventory of our sinful actions, Satan floods our minds with our past sins. He accuses us of sins that we already confessed, and he blames us for sins that we never did. Hence, we begin to focus on Satan's thoughts and ignore the Holy Spirit's voice. When Satan accuses us, he confuses us with guilt. Many times, we do not even know how we sinned because of the confusion. Because of our guilt, we begin to doubt that we are Christians. In the Bible, Satan accused Joshua, a high priest of God:

> Then he showed me Joshua the high priest standing before the angel of the LORD, and **Satan standing at his right side to accuse him**. The LORD said to Satan, "**The LORD rebuke you, Satan!** The LORD, who has chosen Jerusalem, rebuke you! Is not this man a burning stick snatched from the fire?" Now Joshua was dressed in filthy clothes as he stood before the angel. The angel said to those who were standing before him, "**Take off his filthy clothes**." Then he said to Joshua, "See, I have taken away your sin, and I will **put rich garments on you**."
> (Zec.3:1-4 NIV)

When Satan accused Joshua, God did three things. God rebuked Satan, forgave Joshua's sins, and clothed him in holiness. First, God rebuked Satan. In other words, God told Satan to stop accusing Joshua and to leave. We must also rebuke Satan when he shouts his accusations against us so that we can hear the Holy Spirit's voice. We should only talk to Satan to rebuke him. Through conviction, the Holy Spirit quietly points out very specific sins in our lives. When the Holy Spirit convicts us, one sin at a time, we experience God's peace as we talk to Him about specific sins:

> If we confess our sins, He is faithful and just **to forgive us our sins and to cleanse us from all unrighteousness**. (1Jn.1:9 NKJV)

Second, God forgives us because we confessed our sins. Even though Satan will still accuse us of these sins, we know that we are forgiven:

> For as the heavens are high above the earth, **so great is His mercy toward those who fear Him**; as <u>far as the east is from the west</u>, so **far has He removed our transgressions from us.** (Ps.103:11-12 NKJV)

Through forgiveness, God removes the guilt from our consciences:

> Just think **how much more the blood of Christ will purify our consciences from sinful deeds** so that we can worship the living God. For by the power of the eternal Spirit, Christ offered himself to God as a perfect sacrifice for our sins. (He.9:14 NLT)

Third, God purifies us. When God purifies us, He removes the desire to do the sins that we confessed. We will no longer do these sins because He promises to help us. Since we do not continue to do these sins, we give Satan no reason to accuse us of them:

> I care very little if I am judged by you or by any human court; indeed, I do not even judge myself. **My conscience is clear, but that does not make me innocent.** It is the Lord who judges me. (1Co.4:6 NIV)

If Christians do not confess their sins, they remain guilty. Therefore, Satan can accuse them; for their sins have not been forgiven. Unlike these Christians, we must confess our sins as soon as the Holy Spirit points them out. For confession removes our guilt:

> **Yet now he has reconciled you to himself through the death of Christ** in his physical body. As a result, he has brought you into his own presence, and **you are holy and blameless as** <u>**you stand before him without a single fault**</u>. (Co.1:22-23 NLT)

Jesus can forgive and remove **all** sins:

> But if we walk in the light as He is in the light, we have fellowship with one another, and <u>**the blood of Jesus**</u> **Christ His Son cleanses us from all sin.** (1Jn.1:7 NKJV)

Since we made an inventory of our sinful actions, we must deal with our sins. We must admit our sins to ourselves and realize that we alone did them. Then, we must confess our sins to God and to another Christian.

For Further Thought:

I find confession difficult because...

1. Are there any good excuses for our sins?

2. Why must we admit our specific sins to ourselves?

3. Why must we confess our specific sins to God?

4. Why must we admit our specific sins to another Christian?

5. Do you want to admit your sins to another person? Why, or why not?

6. What is the difference between temptation and sin?

7. What is the difference between conviction and accusation?

8. Why must a Christian learn to discern?

Memory Verse:
If we confess our sins, he is faithful and just and will forgive us our sins and purify us from all unrighteousness.   1 John 1:9

NOTES:

Step 6

Preparing for Change

STEP 6 *We agree with the Scripture that we are a new creation in Christ and that all God's promises are ours. We wait on Him to change us by the power of the Holy Spirit.*

Grace

In step 1, we realized that we were helpless. In step 2, we asked Jesus to help us. In step 3, we gave God control of our lives. In step 4, we made a list of our sinful actions. In step 5, we admitted our sins. Now, in step 6, we wait for God to change us. Why must we wait for God? Why do we not start to change ourselves? After all, we must change:

> *Nevertheless, the firm foundation of God stands, having this seal, "The Lord knows those who are His," and,* **"Everyone who names the name of the Lord is to abstain from wickedness."** (2Ti.2:19 NASB)

Before we were Christians, we could not obey God by our own strength. Why would we think we could change ourselves now? We can't. Instead, we are changed to become like God because of the grace which came through Christ. When we believed in Jesus, we received grace:

> *For* **the law** *was given through Moses, but* **grace and truth came through Jesus Christ**. (Jn.1:17 NKJV; Ro.1:5)

Grace came to mankind when Jesus came to the earth. Grace is a gift:

> *For* **by grace you have been saved** *through faith, and this is not your own doing;* **it is** <u>**the gift of God**</u>—**not the result of works**, *so that no one may boast.* (Eph.2:8-10 NRSV; Ro.11:5-6)

God's grace gives us the strength to say "No!" to sin:

> *"For* **the grace of God** *that brings salvation has appeared to all men.* <u>**It teaches us to say "No" to ungodliness and worldly passions,**</u> *and to live self-controlled,* **upright and godly lives** <u>**in this present age**</u>, *who gave himself for us* **to redeem us from all wickedness** *and to purify for himself*

a people that are his very own, eager to do what is good."
(Ti.2:11-14 NIV)

Grace changes our lives. Because we have grace, we no longer keep on sinning. Rather, we live to please God:

> **For sin shall not be your master**, *because you are not under law, but* **under grace**. (Ro 6:14 NIV)

In the Bible, the Holy Spirit is called the Spirit of grace:

> *Who has insulted* **the Spirit of grace***?* (He.10:29 NIV)

Therefore, we have grace because the Holy Spirit lives in us. He changes us and makes us act more and more like Christ:

> *As for us, we can't help but thank God for you, dear brothers and sisters loved by the Lord. We are always thankful that* **God chose you to be among the first to experience salvation**—*a salvation* **that came through the Spirit** <u>**who makes you holy**</u> *and through your belief in the truth.* (2Th.2:13 NLT)

WAITING ON GOD

Imagine that a man was drowning because he could not swim. His arms beat the water to keep his head up. However, the lifeguard stayed a few feet from the man. Finally, the man gave up struggling. Then, the lifeguard grabbed him and pulled him to the shore. If the lifeguard tried to save the man while he struggled to keep his head above water, the man would have drowned the lifeguard. The drowning man's efforts to save himself prevented the lifeguard from saving him.

Before we were Christians, we beat at our sins. In other words, we tried to stop them by ourselves. But we found that we could not obey the Law and stop sinning. We were not righteous. A righteous person does what is right according to God:

> *For merely listening to the law doesn't make us right with God.* **It is obeying the law that makes us right in his sight.** (Ro.2:13 NLT)

As long as we tried to be righteous on our own, God could not help us. Therefore, we must not try to stop our sins by our own strength. Rather, we must ask God to change our lives. Once we ask God for help, we must wait for Him. In this way, God makes us righteous:

> *You who **are trying** to be justified **by law** have been **alienated from Christ**; you have **fallen away from grace**. But **by faith we eagerly await** through **the Spirit** the **righteousness for which we hope**.*
>
> (Ga.5:4-5 NIV)

We will lose God's help if we try to obey God's Law by our own strength. We must ask God for help and wait for the Holy Spirit to stop our sins. Because we have asked God, we expect that today we will not do the same sins that we confessed yesterday:

> *If **by the Spirit** you put to death the deeds of the body, **you will live**. For **as many as are led by the Spirit** of God, these are sons of God.*
>
> (Ro.8:13-14 NKJV)

Because the Holy Spirit lives in us, we believe that today will be different. We expect God to answer our prayers for help. The Spirit of grace will help us, but we must be humble enough to ask. Humble Christians ask God for help. Then, they expect God's strength to help them say "No!" to sin:

> *All of you, clothe yourselves with humility toward one another, because, "God opposes the proud but **gives grace to the humble**." Humble yourselves, therefore, under God's mighty hand, that **he may lift you up in due time**. Cast all your anxiety on him because he cares for you.*
>
> (1Pe.5:5-7 NIV)

If God stopped our sins before we asked, we might think that we changed our own lives. Therefore, God waits until we know our weaknesses and call out to Him for help. Then, He gives us His grace:

> *The everlasting God, the LORD, The Creator of the ends of the earth, Neither faints nor is weary. His understanding is unsearchable. **He gives power to the weak**, And to those who have no might **He increases strength**. Even the youths shall faint and be weary, And the young men shall utterly fall, But **those who wait on the LORD Shall renew their strength**; They shall mount up with wings like eagles, They shall run and **not be weary**, They shall walk and **not faint**.*
>
> (Isa.40:28-31 NKJV)

If we are still trying to stop sinning on our own, we are not relying on God. We rely on God by asking Him for help and by waiting for Him to help us. Then, the Holy Spirit will give us the strength to stop our sins.

THE CAUSE OF HABITUAL SINS

When we became Christians, some of our sins were strong and hard to stop. Often, demons control these sinful habits in a new Christian's life. A person cannot stop these types of sinful habits unless he deals with Satan and his demons:

> Finally, **be strong in the Lord and in the strength of His might**. Put on the full armor of God, so that you will be able to stand firm against the schemes of the devil. For **our struggle is not against flesh and blood, but against the <u>rulers</u>, against the <u>powers</u>, against the <u>world forces of this darkness</u>, against the <u>spiritual forces of wickedness</u>** in the heavenly places. (Eph.6:10-12 NASB)

Not all sins are poor choices. Sometimes, demons cause sins. Only God can free a person from these demonic sins. For this reason, Jesus told us to pray:

> And **do not lead us into temptation**, But **deliver us from the evil one**. (Mt 6:13 NKJV)

Satan will tempt all Christians. But he will not control Christians. We will study different levels of demonic control: seared consciences, footholds, and strongholds. If a person sears his conscience, he makes a foothold. Footholds can become strongholds.

SEARING OF THE CONSCIENCE

A Christian must not give in to a temptation. If a churchgoer (a person who attends church but does not have the Holy Spirit controlling him) or a new Christian does cave in to temptation, he will find the sin about 30% easier to do the next time Satan tempts him. The churchgoer becomes about 5 % weaker every time that he gives in to the temptation. Sooner or later, this churchgoer will always give in to the sin when he is tempted. At this point, he no longer feels guilty for that sin. He has seared (destroyed) part of his conscience:

> Such teachings come through hypocritical liars, **whose consciences have been seared** as with a hot iron. (1Ti.4:2 NIV)

A churchgoer can also sear part of his conscience if he watches other people sin. For example, if a person watches TV, he sees how the world usually sins in a certain situation. When the churchgoer is in that situation, he responds just like the characters on TV and sins like the world. He does not feel guilty because he has watched others do the sin so many times. The book of Proverbs says:

> Can a man scoop a flame into his lap and **not have his clothes catch on fire**? Can he walk on hot coals **and not blister his feet**?
> (Pr.6:27-28 NLT)

If a churchgoer often thinks about a sin, he will not feel guilt when he does it. Rather, it will be easy for him to do it:

> For **as he thinketh** in his heart, **so is he**. (Pr.23:7 KJV)

If he continues to do a sin, he will not feel guilty any more for that sin. God commands Christians to think about good things:

> Finally, brethren, whatever is **true**, whatever is **honorable**, whatever is **right**, whatever is **pure**, whatever is **lovely**, whatever is of good **repute**, if there is **any excellence** and if anything **worthy of praise**, **let your mind dwell on these things.** (Php.4:8 NASB)

Since Christians think about good things, they will do good things. In this way, Christians make their consciences sensitive to right and wrong. They will listen to their consciences and obey God:

> Do not get drunk with wine, for that is debauchery; but **be filled with the Spirit,** (Eph.5:18 NRSV)

In conclusion, a churchgoer can sear part of his conscience in two ways. First, he sears his conscience when he watches other people sin. Second, he sears his conscience when he does a sin over and over again. A Christian should never sear his conscience. If a churchgoer continues to sear his conscience, he will give Satan a foothold in his life.

FOOTHOLDS

If a person does a sin over and over again, he creates a foothold. When a person has a foothold, he might want to do the right thing, but he continues to do the sin because he has lost control:

> For I know that **nothing good dwells within me**, that is, in my flesh. **I can will what is right, but I cannot do it.** For **I do not do the good** I want, but the evil I do not want is what I do. Now if I do what I do not

want, it is no longer I that do it, but sin that dwells within me.
(Ro.7:18-20 NRSV)

Before Paul was a Christian, Satan had footholds in Paul's life. Like Paul, some churchgoers have footholds. They do not choose to sin all by themselves anymore. Rather, they always do the same sin because a demon now has the power to make them sin. In other words, a demon controls these people from outside their bodies. The sin is now a strong habit:

> *Those who oppose him he must gently instruct, in the hope that God will grant them repentance leading them to a knowledge of the truth, and that they will come to their senses and* **escape from the trap of the devil, who has taken them captive to do his will.** (2Ti.2:25-26 NIV)

Some footholds are overeating, drunkenness, lusting, lying, and gossiping. According to the Bible, a foothold (sinful habit) is a sin that traps a churchgoer or, even possibly, a new Christian:

> *Therefore, since we have so great a cloud of witnesses surrounding us, let us also lay aside every encumbrance and* **the sin which so easily entangles us,** *and let us run with endurance the race that is set before us, fixing our eyes on Jesus, the author and perfecter of faith.*
> (He.12:1 NASB)

Some people always give in to a temptation. These people try to stop the sin, but they cannot stop it. They do not know that a demon has taken control of them through the sin. At this point, they realize that they are not in control of themselves:

> *We know that the law is spiritual; but I am unspiritual,* **sold as a slave to sin.** *I do not understand what I do. For what I want to do I do not do, but what I hate I do. And if I do what I do not want to do, I agree that the law is good. As it is,* **it is no longer I myself who do it, but it is sin living in men.** (Ro.7:14-17 NIV)

If a person keeps on searing his conscience toward a sin, he will create a foothold. A common foothold for churchgoers is bitterness (unforgiveness):

> *"In your anger do not sin": Do not let the sun go down while you are still angry, and* **do not give the devil a foothold.** (Eph.4:25-26 NIV)

When churchgoers will not forgive others, they create a foothold. They feel that they have the right to be bitter. These churchgoers refuse to listen to the Holy Spirit when He speaks to their consciences. In this way, they give Satan control of their lives. Through this foothold, Satan has destroyed many churches. In conclusion, some people in the church have footholds. Demons control them and now make them sin.

STRONGHOLDS

A foothold can become a stronghold. A Christian will never **create** a stronghold in his life. When a person has a stronghold, the demon actually lives in him. However, the person is not demon possessed, 100% controlled. Rather, the demon only controls one area of the person's life. The demon forces the person to do a specific sin and corrupts his mind to horrible extremes. Because of the stronghold, the person destroys himself and others through his sin:

> But **these men revile the things which they do not understand**; and the things which they know **by instinct**, like unreasoning animals, **by these things they are destroyed.** (Jude 1:10 NASB)

If a person has a stronghold, a demon controls him in that area. Over time, the demon gains control over other areas of the person's life. If a churchgoer or new Christian has a stronghold, he must not lose hope. Christ can break the stronghold. Once Christ lives in you, He takes control of your life. Therefore, a demon cannot remain in you at the same time as Christ:

> You are of God, little children, and have overcome them, because **He who is _in you_ is greater than he who is in the world.** (1Jn.4:4 NKJV)

Mature Christians can break a new Christian's stronghold. First, they must command the demon to leave. Then, they must teach the Bible's principles concerning the sin and how to overcome the sin:

> Indeed, we live as human beings, but we do not wage war according to human standards; for **the weapons of our warfare are not merely human**, but they have **divine power to destroy strongholds.**
> (2Co.10:4 NRSV)

People with strongholds could be pedophiles, rapists, murderers, alcoholics, anorexics, etc. Christians must realize that certain demons cause certain strongholds. For example, the Bible talks about the demon of prostitution (Ho.5:4; Ho.4:12), the demon of impurity (Ze.13:2), the demon of dizziness from drinking (Isa.19:14), and the demon of depression

(1Sa.12:26). A person cannot remove a stronghold by his own strength. He needs Christ to come into his life and take control of him.

Destroying Strongholds

If a churchgoer has a foothold, he must make Jesus the Lord of his life by giving Him full control. Then, Jesus will remove the foothold. If a new Christian has a foothold, he must confess the foothold. Some people have strongholds when they become Christians. However, they cannot remove their strongholds by confession. Rather, they can be freed if they follow some important truths. Christ came to free us from Satan's power:

> *The one who practices sin is of the devil; for the devil has sinned from the beginning.* ***The Son of God appeared for this purpose, to destroy the works of the devil.*** (1Jn.3:8 NASB)

Once we are Christians, Jesus has saved us from Satan and his demons:

> ***For he has rescued us from the dominion of darkness*** *and brought us into the kingdom of the Son he loves, in whom we have redemption, the forgiveness of sins.* (Co.1:13-14 NIV; Ac.26:17-18)

There are some things that must be done to break Satan's control over a stronghold.

1. Christ — Lord of Our Lives

Some people in church have strongholds because Jesus is not their Lord (Master). He is only their Savior. These people are like a man in the Bible:

> *"When **an evil spirit leaves a person**, it goes into the desert, seeking rest but finding none. Then it says, 'I will return to the person I came from.' So it returns and finds **its former home empty, swept, and in order**. Then the spirit finds seven other spirits more evil than itself, and **they all enter the person and live there**. And so that person is worse off than before. That will be the experience of this evil generation."* (Mt.12:43-45 NLT)

Someone commanded the demon to leave the man. However, the man could not keep demons out because Jesus did not live in him. Therefore, other demons entered the man. Like this man, some people trade one stronghold for a different stronghold. For example, some people give up smoking but then begin to overeat. How can a person get rid of his stronghold? He must make Jesus Christ his Lord (Master). When we became Christians, Jesus entered us. From that time on, Jesus is our master. We obey Jesus because He controls us completely:

> *I pray that out of his glorious riches he may strengthen you **with power through his Spirit** in your inner being, **so that Christ may dwell in your hearts through faith**.* (Eph.3:16-17 NIV)

Jesus is our Lord, and He lives in us. Therefore, our strongholds are gone. Demons cannot live in us because Jesus lives in us:

> *In that day you will know that I am in My Father, and you in Me, and **I in you**.* (Jn.14:19 NASB)

The Almighty God lives in every Christian:

> *Jesus answered and said to him, "If anyone loves Me, he will keep My word; and **My Father** will love him, and **We will come to him** and **make Our home with him**.* (Jn.14:23 NKJV)

Because Jesus Christ lives in us, we have God inside of us:

> *For in Christ **all the fullness of the Deity** lives in bodily form, and **you have been given fullness in Christ**, who is the head over every power and authority.* (Co.2:9-10 NIV)

Therefore, a person gets rid of a stronghold by first making Jesus Lord of his life.

2. THE BATTLE WAS ALREADY WON

When Jesus Christ died on the cross, He overcame Satan and his demons:

> *In this way, **he disarmed the spiritual rulers and authorities**. He shamed them publicly **by his victory over them on the cross**.* (Co.2:15 NLT)

When Jesus rose from the dead, He forced Satan and his demons to obey Him:

> *It saves you **by the resurrection of Jesus Christ**, who has gone into heaven and is at God's right hand— **with angels, authorities and powers in submission to him**.* (1Pe.3:21-22 NIV)

Therefore, Jesus is stronger than Satan. Because Jesus lives in us, we can overcome strongholds:

> *Little children, you are from God, and* **have conquered them;** *for* **the one who is in you is greater than the one who is in the world**.
> (1Jn.4:4 NRSV)

Because Jesus lives in a Christian, new Christians can be freed of their strongholds. Christians will not get other strongholds, because Jesus protects them from Satan and his demons:

> *We know that* **those who are born of God** *do not sin, but* **the one** *who* **was born of God protects them**, *and* **the evil one does not touch them**.
> (1Jn.5:18 NRSV)

Satan has no rights over a Christian. We are not only protected from Satan but now have power over Satan:

> *Behold, I give you the authority to trample on serpents and scorpions, and* **over all the power of the enemy, and nothing shall by any means hurt you**. *Nevertheless do not rejoice in this,* **that the spirits are subject to you**, *but rather rejoice because your names are written in heaven.*
> (Lk.10:19-20 NKJV)

Therefore, Jesus overcame Satan and his demons. Jesus gave us authority over Satan. Jesus gave us the weapons that can free other people from their strongholds:

> **The weapons we fight with** *are not the weapons of the world. On the contrary,* **they** **have divine power to demolish strongholds**.
> (2Co.10:4 NIV)

3. CONFRONTING SATAN

Jesus removed our strongholds. But we must not sin in those areas again. We must not be afraid of Satan but must stand against Satan:

> *Put on all of God's armor so that* **you will be able to stand firm against** *all strategies of the devil.*
> (Eph 6:11 NLT)

If a new Christian does not deal with Satan, Satan will seek to destroy him:

> *Be self-controlled and alert. Your enemy the devil prowls around like a roaring lion looking for someone to devour.* **Resist him, standing firm in the faith**, *because you know that your brothers throughout the world are undergoing the same kind of sufferings.*
> (1Pe.5:8-9 NIV)

We need to believe that God will help us stand, for He promised:

> *The temptations in your life are no different from what others experience. And God is faithful.* **He will not allow the temptation to be more than you can stand.** *When you are tempted, he will show you a way out* **so that you can endure.** (1Co.10:13 NLT)

We must not be afraid but must stand up against sin and Satan. God promises to give us power:

> *To his own master he stands or falls;* **and <u>he will stand</u>, for <u>the Lord is able to make him stand</u>.** (Ro.14:4 NASB)

Even though God promises to help us stand, we need to be alert and ready to deal with Satan when he comes against us:

> *Keep* **alert**, **stand firm** *in your faith, be* **courageous**, *be* **strong**. (1Co.16:13 NRSV)

We stand by using the authority that Jesus gave us over Satan:

> *Truly I say to you,* **whatever you bind on earth shall have been bound in heaven**; *and whatever you* **loose on earth shall have been loosed in heaven.** (Mt.18:18 NASB)

We bind Satan from acting and command him to release his hold on people. Whenever Satan tempts us, we must command him to leave us. Then, we are empowered to stop sinning. Jesus showed us how to deal with Satan:

> *Jesus said to him,* **"Away from me, Satan!** (Mt.4:10 NIV; Mt.16:23)

Therefore, we must use Christ's authority to stop Satan. Satan wants to trap us in sins again.

4. FILLED WITH THE SPIRIT

In our past lives, we focused on sinful things. However, with God's help, we can change:

> *Don't be drunk with wine, because that will ruin your life.* **Instead, be filled with the Holy Spirit.** (Eph.5:18 NLT)

New Christians must not seek after worldly things. Rather, they must seek after God. Otherwise, Satan will control their lives again. Since Christ controls us, He will show us the sins that are still in our lives. Then, we must daily ask God for strength. Because of God's strength, we will say "No!" to sin:

> *Put to death, therefore, whatever belongs to your earthly nature: sexual immorality, impurity, lust, evil desires and greed, which is idolatry. Because of these, the wrath of God is coming. **You <u>used to</u> walk in these ways**, in the life you <u>once lived</u>. **But now you must rid yourselves of all such things as** these: anger, rage, malice, slander and filthy language from your lips.* (Co.1:5-8 NIV)

The Holy Spirit gives us strength to say "No!" to sin. He also changes us so that we want to be like Christ.

> *I pray that, according to the riches of his glory, **he may grant that you may be strengthened in your inner being with power through his Spirit**, and that Christ may dwell in your hearts through faith.* (Eph.3:16-17 NRSV)

We must put our sins to death by the Holy Spirit's power:

> *Therefore, dear brothers and sisters, you have no obligation to do what your sinful nature urges you to do. For if you live by its dictates, you will die. But **if through the power of the Spirit you put to death the deeds of your sinful nature**, you will live.* (Ro.8:13 NLT)

Once the Holy Spirit lives in us, we will no longer live for sin:

> *So I say, live by the Spirit, and **you will not gratify the desires of the sinful nature**.* (Ga.5:16 NIV)

Therefore, we must ask God for help. Then, we wait and rely on Him to give us the strength. We must trust that the Holy Spirit will give us the strength to say "No" to sin:

> *Let us therefore **come boldly to the throne of grace**, that we may obtain mercy and **find grace to help in time of need**.* (He.4:16 NKJV)

For Further Thought:

At times we must wait because...

1. What is the difference between law and grace?

2. Why must we know that grace is a free gift?

3. What is the difference between trying by our own strength and relying on God's strength?

4. How do people sear their consciences?

5. Why must Christians know about footholds and strongholds?

6. How does a person get rid of footholds?

7. How does a person become free from a stronghold?

8. How do we remain free from footholds and strongholds?

Memory Verse:
You, dear children, are from God and have overcome them, because the one who is in you is greater than the one who is in the world. 1 John 4:4

NOTES:

Step 7

A Life of Humility

Step 7 *We humbly ask God for His strength to overcome all temptations, for His protection from Satan, and for His cleansing from the desire to sin.*

Prayer: Releasing God's Power

By this time, we have learned that we rely on God. Apart from God, we are nothing; for we are not strong enough to change ourselves:

> *Remain in me, and I will remain in you. For a branch cannot produce fruit if it is severed from the vine, and* **you cannot be fruitful unless you remain in me**. *"Yes, I am the vine; you are the branches. Those who remain in me, and I in them, will produce much fruit.* **For apart from me you can do nothing**. (Jn.15:4-5 NLT)

Some people know that they need help. They could get help, but they are too proud to ask. We know we need help because we cannot stop sinning. However, we too must be humble enough to ask. God will help everyone who asks Him:

> **All of you, clothe yourselves with humility** *toward one another, because, "God opposes the proud but gives grace to the humble."* **"Humble yourselves**, *therefore,* **under God's mighty hand**, *that* **he may lift you up** **in due time**. *Cast all your anxiety on him because he cares for you."* (1 Pe.5:6-7 NIV)

Prayer is an act of humility. When we pray, we are asking the Almighty God to help us. We do not know how God will help us, but we know that He has promised to help us. When we pray, we reach out to God for supernatural help. For example, a father watches his son trying to open his toy box. The father knows that the son cannot lift the lid. But the father waits until his son gives up and asks for help. God is like this father.

God wants to help His children. Many times, we struggle with all our strength against sin. But we do not overcome our sins because we refuse to humble ourselves and ask God for help:

> You want something but don't get it. You kill and covet, but you cannot have what you want. You quarrel and fight. **You do not have, because you do not ask God.** (Ja.4:2 NIV)

Jesus died to set us free from sin. Since He was willing to suffer and die for us, He will also give us the help that we need:

> He who did not withhold his own Son, but gave him up for all of us, **will he not with him also give us <u>everything else</u>**? (Ro.8:32 NRSV)

God knows the future. He knows what we need before we ask Him. But He waits until we ask:

> "And when you are praying, do not use meaningless repetition as the Gentiles do, for they suppose that they will be heard for their many words. "So do not be like them; **for your Father knows what you need before you ask Him.** (Mt.6:7-8 NASB)

If God helped us before we asked, we might think that we overcame sin by ourselves. In the Bible, God says to ask with thanksgiving. By thanking Him, while we ask, we recognize that God is the One Who answers our prayers:

> Do not be anxious about anything, but in every situation, **by prayer** and petition, **<u>with thanksgiving</u>, present your requests to God.** (Php.4:6 NIV; 1Th.5:16-18; 1Ti.2:1)

Sometimes, we must pray for a period of time before God stops a sin in our lives. God, by making us wait, helps us realize that only He can give us the strength to stop our sins. As we wait, we continue to pray for God's strength. We must not give up:

> Jesus told his disciples a parable to show them that they **should always pray and not give up**. (Lk.18:1 NIV)

There are many reasons to pray. Also, there are different ways to pray. When we pray, we must let the Holy Spirit guide us:

> And **<u>pray in the Spirit</u>** on **<u>all occasions</u>** with **<u>all kinds of prayers</u>** and **requests.** With this in mind, be alert and always keep on praying for all the saints. (Eph.6:18 NIV; Jude 1:12)

When we pray, we must ask the Holy Spirit to lead us. He will give us the words to pray. Therefore, we will know what we must ask for:

> In the same way **the Spirit also helps our weakness; for we do not know how to pray as we should**, but the Spirit Himself intercedes for us with groanings too deep for words; and He who searches the hearts knows what the mind of the Spirit is, because **He intercedes for the saints according to the will of God.** (Ro.8:26-27 NASB)

Since the Holy Spirit guides us, we will pray according to God's will. Only when our requests are in line with God's will, can He answer our prayers:

> This is the confidence which we have before Him, that, **if we ask anything according to His will, He hears us**. And if we know that He hears us in whatever we ask, **we know that we have the requests which we have asked from Him**. (1Jo.5:14-15 NRSV)

Because God desires us to be holy, we can be sure that He will answer. When God gives us the strength to stop a sin, we must give Him the praise. We must give God all the glory for the change that He has made in our lives:

> And I will do whatever you ask in my name, **so that the Son may bring glory to the Father**. You may ask me **for anything in my name**, and I will do it. (Jn.14:13-14 NIV)

Therefore, we must humble ourselves by asking God for help. When He helps us, we praise Him for what He has done.

A Christian's Response to Temptation

Satan tempted Christ until He died. Therefore, Satan will tempt us until the day that we die. Satan wants to trap us in sin:

> The **temptations in your life** are **no different from what others experience.** (1Co.10:13 NLT)

When Satan tempts us, he presents us with different ways to disobey God. The following verses describe how Satan tempts us:

> But **each one is tempted** when **he is drawn away by his own desires** and enticed. Then, **when desire has conceived**, it gives birth to sin; and sin, when it is full-grown, **brings forth death.** (Ja.1:13-15 NKJV)

According to these verses, Satan tempts a person, the person desires to sin, he does the sin, and then he dies. In these verses, the person's sinful nature is still alive. Therefore, he is not a Christian. Christians have died to their sinful nature:

> Those who belong to Christ Jesus **have crucified the sinful nature with its passions and desires.** (Ga.5:24 NIV)

Because the person described in James 1:13-15 has sin that causes eternal death, this person could not have been a Christian. Christians have eternal life:

> **We know** that we **have passed from death to life** because we love one another. Whoever does not love abides in death. (1Jn.3:14 NRSV)

Christ was tempted like we are. Therefore, He knows how Satan will tempt us:

> For we do not have a High Priest who cannot sympathize with our weaknesses, but **was in all points tempted as we are, <u>yet without sin</u>.** (He.4:15 NKJV)

Before we were Christians, Satan tempted us, and we naturally sinned. Once we are Christians, Satan will still tempt us, but Christ now lives in us. Because Christ, Who cannot sin, lives in us, He will help us so that we will not keep on sinning:

> I have been crucified with Christ; and **it is no longer I who live, but Christ lives in me.** (Ga.2:20 NASB)

We are different than the people in the Old Testament because Jesus Christ now lives in us:

> "As you, **<u>Father, are in me</u>** and **<u>I am in you</u>**, **may they also be in us**, so that the world may believe that you have sent me. (Jn.17:20-21 NRSV; Jn.14:20;; Co.2:9-10)

God and Jesus are one being. Therefore, our holy God lives in us:

> Whoever confesses that Jesus is the Son of God, **God abides in him, and he in God.** (1Jn.4:15 NKJV)

God does not have a sinful nature, for He is holy. Once God's Spirit lives in us, we have a new divine nature:

> His divine power has **given us everything we need for life and godliness** through our knowledge of him who called us by his own glory and goodness. Through these he has given us his very great and precious

> promises, so that through them **you may participate in the divine nature** and escape the corruption in the world caused by evil desires. (2Pe.1:3-4 NIV)

Unlike the man in James 1:13-15, who sinned because of his sinful nature, when Satan tempts us, our divine nature wants to please God. We do not sin; and we do not die. We do not want to sin because a change in our nature alters our desires. For example, I do not like liver; but my wife cooks it because it is good for us. My wife never has to say, "Don't sneak any liver out of the fridge." I would not choose to eat liver because I do not like it. When I received God's holy nature, all my sins became like liver to me. I naturally stopped sinning because I lost my taste for it. When we confess our sins to God, He changes our desires. Therefore, we do not want to do those sins again. In other words, since we have a holy nature, we begin to lose our taste for our sins:

> **Consider it pure joy,** my brothers, whenever you face **trials** [temptations] **of many kinds,** because you know that the **testing of your faith develops** perseverance. Perseverance must finish its work so **that you may be mature and complete,** not lacking anything. (Ja.1:2-4 NIV)

Once we have the divine nature, temptations lose their power over us. Therefore, we will not choose to sin when Satan tempts us. However, God allows Satan to continue to tempt us so that we will grow stronger. God wants us to be able to say "No!" to strong temptations. For example, a weight lifter starts with light weights. But he does not lift the same weight forever. Rather, he increases the weight so that his strength will increase. When we become Christians, temptations do not stop, for God wants us to learn to trust in Him. In conclusion, before we were Christians, our sinful nature was alive, and we wanted to sin when Satan tempted us. Now that we are Christians, we have God's holy nature. Therefore, we do not want to sin when Satan tempts us.

GOD CONTROLS THE TEMPTER

God is sovereign. In other words, God is more powerful than anyone or anything. Since God is sovereign, He controls Satan. God promises us that He will protect us from Satan:

> But the Lord is faithful, and **He will strengthen and protect you from the evil one.** We have **confidence in the Lord** concerning you, that you **are doing and will continue to do** what we command.
> (2Th.3:3-4 NASB)

God puts a hedge around us to protect us. A hedge is a spiritual boundary that Satan cannot break. In the Bible, God put a hedge around Job:

> "Does Job fear God for nothing?" Satan replied. **"Have you not put a hedge around him** and his **household** and **everything** he has?
> (Job 1:9-10 NIV)

Satan could not break the hedge that protected Job, his family, and his things. Hence, Satan asked God to remove the hedge. God said:

> Then the LORD said to Satan, "Behold, **all that he has is in your power, only do not put forth your hand on him.** So Satan departed from the presence of the LORD. (Job 1:12 NASB)

God had to give Satan permission to tempt Job before he could touch Job in anyway. Therefore, God moved the hedge that protected Job's family and things. But God did not give Satan free reign. Rather, God kept a hedge around Job himself. Satan killed Job's family and stole everything he had. Satan did this to tempt Job to curse God. However, Job withstood the temptation and did not curse God. God used the hedge around Job to limit where Satan could tempt him. Later, Satan came before God. This time, he asked God to remove the hedge around Job himself. God said:

> The LORD said to Satan, "Very well, **he is in your power; only spare his life."** So Satan went out from the presence of the LORD, and **inflicted loathsome sores on Job** from the sole of his foot to the crown of his head.
> (Job 2:6-7 NRSV)

When Satan got permission, he made Job sick and then sent three friends to accuse and discourage him. But Job still did not curse God. God had limited Satan once again by keeping the hedge around Job's life. Therefore, Job did not sin because God limited the area where Satan could tempt him. God divided the temptation of Job into two parts so that Job would not be tempted beyond what he could take. Today, God puts hedges around us. Satan cannot break these hedges. Satan must ask God to remove these hedges before he can tempt us:

> No temptation has seized you except what is common to man. And **God is faithful**; he will not **let you be tempted beyond what you can bear.**

(1Co.10:13 NIV)

Therefore, God removes our hedges only when He gives us the strength to say "No!" to the temptation.

In the New Testament, God put hedges around His people as well. Before Satan could tempt Peter, Satan had to ask God for permission:

> And the Lord said, "Simon, Simon! Indeed, **Satan has asked for you**, that **he may sift you as wheat**. (Lk.22:31 NKJV)

God gave Satan permission to test Peter's commitment to Christ. When Satan tempted Peter, Peter sinned. Peter sinned because he did not have the Holy Spirit living in him. Remember that it is the Holy Spirit Who gives us the divine nature. The Holy Spirit could only live in people after Jesus rose from the dead:

> By this he meant **the Spirit**, whom those who believed in him **were later to receive**. Up to that time **the Spirit had not been given**, since Jesus had not yet **been glorified**. (Jn.7:39 NIV)

When we received the Holy Spirit, we received His power:

> "Do not leave Jerusalem, but **wait for the gift** my Father promised, which you have heard me speak about. . . You **will receive power when the Holy Spirit has come upon you**; and you shall be My witnesses both in Jerusalem, and in all Judea and Samaria, and even to the remotest part of the earth." (Ac.1:4, 8 NASB)

Once the Holy Spirit lives in us with His power, we are stronger than both sin and Satan:

> Little children, you are from God, and **have conquered them**; for the one **who is in you is greater** than the one who is in the world. (1Jn.4:4 NRSV)

Our confidence is not in our own ability, but in God. He has promised to protect us and give us the power to stand against Satan:

> But **the Lord is faithful**, and **He will strengthen and protect you from the evil one**. We have **confidence in the Lord concerning you, that you are doing and will continue** to do what we command.
> (2Th.3:3-4 NASB)

Even though God made the promise, we must believe that we have the Holy Spirit's power:

> With all of these, take **the shield of faith**, with which you will be able to quench **all the flaming arrows of the evil one**. (Eph.6:16 NRSV)

The flaming arrows are Satan's temptations. Our shield is our faith in God's promises to protect us. If we believe that we have God's power, when Satan tempts us, we will tell him to leave in Jesus' Name. Our faith is in Christ: He freed us from sin and Satan:

> But the Son of God came **to destroy the works of the devil**. Those who have been born into God's family **do not make a practice of sinning**, <u>because God's life is in them</u>. So **they can't keep on sinning**, because they are children of God. (1Jn.3:8-9 NLT)

Only Jesus can keep us safe from the devil and his temptations:

> We know that <u>anyone</u> born of God **does not continue to sin**; <u>**the one**</u> who **was born of God keeps him safe**, and the evil one **cannot harm him**. (1Jn.5:18 NIV)

Therefore, God controls Satan. God limits how much Satan can tempt us. Because the Holy Spirit lives in us, we have God's strength. Therefore, we can refuse to sin when Satan tempts us:

> And I give them eternal life, and **they shall never perish**; neither shall anyone **snatch them out of My hand**. **My Father**, who has given them to Me, **is greater than all**; and **no one is able to snatch them out of My Father's hand**. I and My Father are one. (Jn.10:28-29 NKJV)

Pray for Help

Before Christ died, He faced the greatest temptation of His life. God planned that Jesus would die on a cross. However, Jesus did not look forward to His death for two reasons. First, Jesus would feel all the pain when He was beaten and crucified. Second, Jesus would be rejected by His Father for the first time. For sin separates a person from God. Throughout His ministry, Jesus referred to God as His Father. But when Jesus took our sins upon Himself, He said:

> And about the ninth hour Jesus cried out with a loud voice, saying, "Eli, Eli, lama sabachthani?" that is, "**My God, My God, why have You forsaken Me?**" (Mt.27:46 NKJV)

Jesus did not want the pain. He did not want to be rejected by His Father. Still, He willingly died. The night before Jesus died, He prayed:

> He went a little farther and **fell on His face, and prayed**, saying, "O My Father, if it is possible, let this cup pass from Me; nevertheless, not as I will, but as You will.". . . **Again, a second time, He went away and prayed**,

> saying, "O My Father, if this cup cannot pass away from Me unless I drink it, Your will be done."... **So He left them, went away again, and prayed the third time**, saying the same words.
>
> (Mt.26:39-44 NKJV)

Jesus prayed three times about His death. When He prayed, He asked God if there was another way to save mankind from their sins. Jesus prayed with all His heart, but since there was no other way, He was willing to die for us:

> Then he withdrew from them about a stone's throw, knelt down, and prayed, "Father, if you are willing, remove this cup from me; yet, not my will but yours be done." Then an angel from heaven appeared to him and gave him strength. **In his anguish he prayed more earnestly**, and **his sweat became like great drops of blood falling down on the ground.**
>
> (Lk.22:41-44 NRSV)

Jesus prayed to prepare Himself for temptation. If Christ needed to pray for strength, then we always need to pray. For we are always tempted:

> For we do not have a high priest who is unable to sympathize with our weaknesses, but **we have one who has been tempted in every way, just as we are— yet was without sin.** Let us then **approach the throne of grace with confidence,** so that we may **receive mercy** and **find grace to help us in our time of need.** (He.4:15-16 NIV)

When we pray, our prayers come before God's throne in heaven. We keep asking God for help because we know that Satan will keep tempting us. Jesus told us to pray:

> And **do not lead us into temptation**, But **deliver us from the evil one**.
>
> (Mt.6:13 NKJV)

Why do we pray "lead us not into temptation" since God does not tempt?

> And remember, when you are being tempted, do not say, "God is tempting me." God is never tempted to do wrong, and **he never tempts anyone else.** (Ja.1:13 NLT)

There are two reasons. First, God controls Satan. Satan cannot do anything if God does not let him. For, God can make sure that Satan does not tempt us in areas where we are weak. Second, God can make us strong so that we will say "No!" to sin. God told us to pray in Matthew 6:13 because we need His help. Therefore, we must be humble enough to ask God for help. Before Jesus died, He warned Peter, James, and John:

> When He arrived at the place, He said to them, **"Pray that you may not enter into temptation."** (Lk.22:40 NASB)

Peter thought that he could say "No!" to sin by his own strength. Peter did not pray; rather, he slept. Jesus warned Peter again:

> At last he stood up again and returned to the disciples, only to find them asleep, **exhausted from grief**. "Why are you sleeping?" he asked them. **"Get up and pray, so that you will not give in to temptation."** (Lk.22:45-46 NLT)

Peter slept while Jesus prayed. He then denied Christ at His trial. Perhaps if the disciples had prayed, God would have helped them:

> Be always on the **watch, and pray** that you may **be able to escape all that is about to happen**, and that you may be able to stand before the Son of Man." (Lk.21:36 NRSV)

Therefore, we must pray to receive God's protection and strength. Then, we will not sin when we are tempted:

> No, **in all these things we are more than conquerors through him** who loved us. For I am convinced that neither death nor life, neither angels nor demons, neither the present nor the future, nor any powers, neither height nor depth, nor anything else in all creation, **will be able to separate us** from the love of God that is in Christ Jesus our Lord. (Ro.8:37-39 NIV)

GOD IS ABLE

We know that we will overcome our sins because of God. God has promised to keep us strong to the end of our lives:

> Now **you have every spiritual gift** you need as you eagerly wait for the return of our Lord Jesus Christ. **He will keep you strong to the end** so that you will be free from all blame on the day when our Lord Jesus Christ returns. **God will do this, for he is faithful to do what he says**, and he has invited you into partnership with his Son, Jesus Christ our Lord. (1Co.1:7-9 NLT)

God cannot lie and will keep every promise that He has made to us:

> "For no matter how many promises God has made, **they are "Yes" in Christ**. And so through him the "Amen" is spoken by us to the glory of God. Now it is <u>**God who makes both us and you stand**</u> **firm in Christ."** (2Co.1:20-21 NIV)

Therefore, we must be like Abraham. God promised Abraham a son, but he and his wife could not have any children. Abraham did **not** pray, "Lord, I must have offended you in some way. I guess you won't keep your promise to give me a child." Rather, Abraham trusted God:

> Yet he did **not waver through unbelief regarding the promise of God**, but **was strengthened in his faith** and gave glory to God, **being fully persuaded that God had power** to do what he had promised.
> (Ro.4:20-21 NIV)

We must be confident that God will help us when we are tempted, for we will still struggle with sins. Before we were Christians, sin was ten times stronger than we were; therefore, we kept losing our battle with sin. Now with the Holy Spirit living in us, we are twice as strong as sin. Hence, we seldom lose. But like Abraham, we must always look to God. God will help us stop sinning one sin at a time:

> **Now may the God of peace make you holy in every way**, and may **your whole spirit and soul and body** be kept blameless until our Lord Jesus Christ comes again. **God will make this happen,** for he who calls you is faithful. (2 Th.5:23-24 NLT)

God promises to help us when we are tempted so that we will not fall into sin:

> **Now to him who is able to keep you from falling**, and to make you stand without blemish in the presence of his glory with rejoicing, to the only God our Savior, **through Jesus Christ** our Lord, be glory.
> (Jude 1:24-25)

Since it is God Who gives us the strength, there is no excuse to fail:

> Who are you to judge another's servant? To his own master he stands or falls. **Indeed, he will be made to stand, for God is able to make him stand.** (Ro.14:4 NKJV)

God has saved us, and He will change us to be like Christ:

> And I am certain that **God, who began the good work within you, will continue his work until it is finally finished** on the day when Christ Jesus returns. (Php.1:6 NLT)

We must remember that we cannot change ourselves. We must continue to call out to God to change us:

> Therefore my dear friends, as you have always obeyed- ... Continue to work out your salvation with fear and trembling, **for it is God who works**

> ***in you** to will and to act according to his good purpose."*
> (Php.2:12-13 NIV)

We were born sinners, but God has made us saints:

> *But **by the grace of God I am what I am**, and his grace to me was not without effect. No, I worked harder than all of them **yet not I, but the grace of God that was with me**.*   (1Co.15:10 NIV)

We know that our lives will be changed by God. Because we know that only God can help us when we are tempted, we humble ourselves by asking God to keep us true to Him to the very end:

> *For I know whom I have believed and **I am convinced that He is able to guard what I have entrusted to Him** until that day."*   (2Ti.1:12 NASB)

Therefore, we walk humbly with God, knowing that He has promised to keep us from sin and to change our lives to be like Him. Therefore, I will place my hope in Him.

For Further Thought:

God waits for us to ask Him for help because...

1. Why must we be humble?

2. How do we get strength from God?

3. Why must we thank God when we pray?

4. Describe what happens when unbelievers are tempted.

5. Describe what happens when Christians are tempted.

6. What does Job's life teach us about temptation?

7. Why do we pray "lead us not into temptation" since God cannot tempt us?

8. How can a Christian not sin?

Memory Verse:
> *We have confidence in the Lord that you are doing and will continue to do the things we command.*   2 Thessalonians 3:4

NOTES:

Step 8

Considering Past Harm

Step 8 *We will ask God to reveal to us all the people we have harmed and to give us the wisdom in order to make amends. We realize that if anyone has harmed us, we will instantly forgive him.*

The Gospel of Peace

Jesus **forgives** our sins and **enables** us to stop continuing the sins that we have confessed to Him. The word "gospel" means "good news." The good news is that through Jesus' two actions we can have peace with God:

> *As shoes for your feet put on whatever will make you ready to proclaim **the gospel of peace**.*   (Eph.6:15 NRSV; Ac.10:36)

When Jesus was born, the angels said that Christians would have peace:

> *"Glory to God in the highest heaven, and **on earth peace** among those whom he favors!"*   (Lk.2:14 NRSV)

When I asked Jesus into my life, I began to experience peace. Before I was a Christian, I offended many people. I did not try to offend people, but rather I offended people because I was self-absorbed. Some of these people still had issues with me after I became a Christian. I knew that God wanted me to make peace with them:

> *If possible, **so far as it depends on you**, be at peace with all men.*   (Ro.12:18 NASB)

In step 8, we list the people whom we have hurt so that in a later step we can make peace with them. To make amends with someone is to repair (fix) the damage that we have caused. Making things right can require anything from giving an apology to paying for financial loss that people have suffered because of us. In this step, we will make a list of people and pray about how to make amends.

People cannot sin without offending someone. An example is Adam and Eve. When Adam and Eve sinned for the first time, they felt both guilt and shame. They offended God. A person feels guilt when he does something wrong. Guilt has to do with the act and the person who commits the act. A person feels shame when he dishonors someone. Shame has to do with the act and how it affects other people. Adam and Eve did not feel guilt or shame before they sinned. When God made man, He commanded him not to eat the forbidden fruit. When Adam and Eve disobeyed God and ate this fruit, their eyes were opened. In other words, they knew what guilt and shame felt like:

> So when the woman saw that the tree was good for food, that it was pleasant to the eyes, and a tree desirable to make one wise, she took of its fruit and ate. She also gave to her husband with her, and he ate. **Then the eyes of both of them were opened,** and they knew that they were naked; and **they sewed fig leaves together and made themselves coverings.** (Ge.3:6-7 NKJV)

Adam and Eve felt guilt because they did something they knew was wrong. They felt shame because they dishonored God by their disobedience. After Adam and Eve disobeyed God, they made clothes from leaves. Both guilt and shame were new feelings for them and made them feel different in a bad way. They made clothes to hide the guilt and shame that they felt inside. Their actions may seem silly. However, today some people turn to alcohol or drugs to hide their guilt and shame. People cannot live with their guilt and shame for long. They must deal with it in some way. In this step, we will deal with our guilt and shame in God's way. By making a list, we will start on our pathway to peace by first admitting to ourselves that we did something wrong. Therefore, admitting to ourselves that we have hurt others is the first step.

GUILT AND SHAME

A person feels guilt when he does wrong. People can react to guilt in three ways: **admit** that they did wrong, **deny** that they did wrong, or **blame** someone else for their wrong actions. Because of guilt, some people deny their actions. They say that they did not do the act. Because of guilt, other people blame someone else for their actions. They might even blame the person whom they have hurt. They say, "He is responsible.

If he did not do that, I would not have done what I did." When people blame others, they are reacting to their sin like Adam and Eve:

> The man said, **"The woman whom you gave to be with me, she gave me** fruit from the tree, and I ate." Then the LORD God said to the woman, "What is this that you have done?" The woman said, **"The serpent tricked me, and I ate."** (Ge.3:12-13 NRSV)

Adam blamed Eve, and Eve blamed the snake. However, Adam and Eve were both guilty because they both disobeyed God. In the past, we may have denied our sins or blamed others for them. But now, we will respond to our sin God's way, by admitting our guilt. In this step, we accept responsibility for how we have offended others. When we make this list, we are admitting our guilt and accepting that no matter what the reasons were for our action, we were in the wrong. We may not control other people's actions, but we are always responsible for how we react. Even if we consider that the other person was 90 percent in the wrong, we still were 10 percent in the wrong and are guilty of wrongdoing—sin. Guilt has to do with the person who committed the act. Therefore, in this step, we will stop denying and blaming. We will admit that we are responsible for our actions and recognize our part in the offense.

When we offend someone, we dishonor him. In other words, we bring shame into our relationship. We can react to shame in three ways: **revenge**—by hurting the person in return; **rejection**—by separating ourselves from the person; or **reconciliation**—by forgiving the person. In this step, we admit that before we were Christians, we dishonored other people. We must make things right with them so that they can forgive us. When God created the earth, He made Adam like Himself; He made Adam in His own image. In this way, God honored Adam. Later, Adam and Eve ate the forbidden fruit that God had reserved for Himself. In this way, they dishonored God and caused a break in their relationship with Him. Because they dishonored God, He sent them out of His garden:

> Therefore the LORD **God sent him out from the garden of Eden**, to cultivate the ground from which he was taken. (Ge.3:23 NASB)

According to His law, God could have killed Adam and Eve. However, God loved them and created mankind to live with Him forever. Therefore, He only sent them out of His garden. Adam and Eve felt shame because they hurt their relationship with God. When we sin, our actions continue to dishonor God. Before we were Christians, we constantly sinned. People looked down on us because of our sins. Because of our sins, these people also looked down on our families and our friends. We brought shame on those we loved. We must also make things right with our families and the friends whom we have shamed. Therefore, we must make amends with the people whom we have shamed by restoring their honor.

Making Things Right with God

When we make a list of those we have hurt, we accept the fact that our sin always dishonors God. When we sin, we dishonor God, and dishonor causes separation. Because of our sin, we were separated from God and could not have a relationship with Him. When we disobeyed God, we dishonored Him and brought shame upon ourselves:

> O LORD, **we** and our kings, our princes and our fathers **are covered with shame** because **we have sinned against you**. (Da.9:8 NIV)

One sin separates a person from God. For example, how many sins did Adam do? One sin! Adam dishonored God once, and God sent him out of the garden forever. How many sins did we do in our lifetime? More than we can count. Our sin separates us from God:

> But your iniquities **have made a separation between you and your God**, And **your sins have hidden His face from you** so that He does not hear.
> (Isa.59:2 NASB)

We need to find a way to restore God's honor in order to end the separation. With man, restoring honor is simple. For example, if, while driving recklessly, a man in Afghanistan kills another man's son in a car accident, he brings shame to the son's family. The family will try to kill the driver to avenge their honor—life for life. The driver goes into hiding while his family tries to agree with the son's family on a blood payment. A blood payment is a sum of money that will restore the family's honor. Once the driver's family pays the money, the driver can come out of hiding as the son's family will no longer try to kill the driver. Therefore, the honor of the son's family is restored by a blood payment. Our sin dishonored God. We need a blood payment to restore God's honor, but what can our blood payment be? God owns everything in the world, and in fact, He made us. Therefore, God will only accept the voluntary death of a perfect man to be our blood payment. Our blood payment must be a man because mankind dishonored God. But the man must be perfect and without shame. You are not perfect and neither am I. Jesus was the only perfect man. He was a man because He was born of a human mother:

> Theirs are the patriarchs, and from them is **traced <u>the human ancestry</u> of Christ, who is God over all**, for ever praised! Amen. (Ro.9:5 NIV)

Jesus did not have a human father because God placed Himself into Mary's egg. Jesus was perfect because He was God. Only God is perfect:

> Therefore you are to be perfect, **as your heavenly Father is perfect**. (Mt 5:48 NASB)

Because God loved us, He became a man (Jesus) and lived a perfect life. Since Jesus never sinned, He never dishonored God. Therefore, He did not deserve to die. Jesus let evil men kill Him in order to be our blood payment to restore God's honor:

> So we are Christ's ambassadors; God is making his appeal through us. We speak for Christ when we plead, **"Come back to God!"** For **God made Christ, who never sinned, to be the offering for our sin**, so that **we could be made right with God** through Christ. (2Co.5:20-21NLT)

We have known good men who have died to save others. However, Jesus is the only perfect man. He let Himself be tortured and killed to restore our honor with God. Through Christ, a way has been made to restore God's honor so that we can regain a relationship with Him:

> For **Christ died for sins once for all**, the righteous for the unrighteous, <u>**to bring you to God**</u>. (1Pe 3:18 NIV; Ro.5:10-11)

Jesus died to make things right between mankind and God. First, we need to believe that Jesus can make peace between us and God and ask Him to be our blood payment:

> Therefore, since **we have been made right in God's sight by faith**, we have **peace with God** because of what Jesus Christ our Lord has done for us. (Ro.5:1 NLT)

Once Jesus is our blood payment, we must invite God's Spirit to live in us. The Holy Spirit restores our relationship with God:

> I pray that from his glorious, unlimited resources **he will empower you with inner strength through his Spirit**. Then **Christ will make his home in your hearts** as you trust in him. (Eph.3:16-17 NLT)

When the Holy Spirit lives in us, our spirits become one with God's Spirit and we have intimate fellowship with God:

> **He who unites himself with the Lord is one with him in spirit.**
> (1Co.6:17 NIV)

Once our spirits become one with God's Spirit, He adopts us to be His children. To be adopted by God as His child is the greatest honor:

> In love **He predestined us to adoption as sons through Jesus Christ** to Himself. (Eph.1:4-5 NASB; 1Jn.3:1)

God is honored when we accept His way to make peace with Him. Therefore, Jesus died as a peace offering to restore God's honor for us. All we have to do is ask Him to be our personal blood payment and invite Him to live in us.

MINISTERS OF RECONCILIATION

Once we have made peace with God, He commands us to bring peace to other people. We must present God's way of peace to the world:

> <u>**All this is from God**</u>, who <u>**reconciled us to himself**</u> through Christ and gave us **the ministry of reconciliation**: that **God was reconciling the world to himself in Christ**, not counting men's sins against them. **And he has committed to us the message of reconciliation**.
> (2Co.5:18-19 NIV)

God also requires that we make peace with the people whom we have dishonored. Remember, you must complete the 12 steps in order. In step 7, we asked God to remove our sins. In step 8, we make peace with the people we have hurt. We must do step 7 first because God must enable us to stop our sin. Otherwise, we will offend people again after we have made things right with them. God wants us to have peace with others, but He also wants us to be holy (stop our sinning):

> "**Make every effort to live in peace with all men** and **to be holy**; without holiness no one will see the Lord." (He.12:14 NIV)

Since God has made peace with us, He asks us to make peace with others. If God lives in us, we will make peace with others a priority:

> He must **turn away from evil** and do good; <u>**he must seek peace**</u> **and pursue it.** for the eyes of the Lord are toward the righteous, and **his ears attend to their prayer**, but the face of the Lord is against those who do

evil. (1Pe.3:11-12 NASB)

The world does not understand why we try to make things right with people. People in the world do not make peace with each other:

> As it is written: "There **is none righteous, no, not one.** . . And **the way of peace they have not known."** (Ro.3:10&17 NKJV)

Since Christians are righteous, they always try to do what is right. Therefore, they will try to make things right with people whom they have hurt:

> **For the kingdom of God** is not food and drink but **righteousness and peace** and joy **in the Holy Spirit.** The one who thus serves Christ is acceptable to God and has human approval. **Let us then pursue what makes for peace** and for mutual up-building. (Ro.14:17-19 NRSV)

Peace is not something we achieve through some form of meditation. Peace can only come through a relationship with God:

> Grace to you and **peace from God our Father** and the Lord Jesus Christ. (1Co.1:3 NKJV)

We do not make peace with people because God commands us. Rather, we naturally make peace because the Holy Spirit lives in us. Our desire to make peace comes from God:

> But the **fruit of the Spirit is** love, joy, **peace**, patience, kindness, goodness, faithfulness, gentleness and self-control. (Ga.5:22 NIV)

The Holy Spirit does not just live in us, but He also controls us. He works in us, causing us to seek peace with other people:

> The mind of sinful man is death, but **the mind controlled by the Spirit is life and peace.** (Ro 8:6 NIV)

The Holy Spirit will give us peace every moment of our day:

> Now may **the Lord of peace** Himself **continually grant you peace in every circumstance.** (2Th.3:16 NASB; Ro.15:13)

Since the Holy Spirit gives us peace, we will try to be at peace with all people in every situation. Therefore, God has made peace with us through Jesus Christ and asks that we do the same:

> **Blessed are the peacemakers**, for they will be **called children of God.** (Mt.5:9 NRSV)

PROCEDURES AND PITFALLS

Before we start to write our list of those we have offended, we must pray and ask God to lead us through the process. Ask God, "Show me whom I have hurt. How did I hurt them?" Then write down what He shows you. There are four different areas in which we could have hurt someone:

> **Material injury:** Did you hurt someone financially? Did you refuse to pay a bill? Did you destroy someone's things? Did you take money from a family member?
>
> **Physical injury:** Did you hurt someone physically? Did you attack someone sexually or physically?
>
> **Emotional injury:** Did you hurt someone's feelings? Did you refuse to help others? Did you say mean things? Did you embarrass your family because of your actions or words?
>
> **Spiritual injury:** Did you refuse to be the leader of your home (wife and children)? Did you hurt someone's faith? Were you critical of someone's faith?

Ask God how we should make things right with each person whom we have offended. Each attempt to make peace will be different because situations and people are unique. We must ask God to protect our minds from Satan. Satan will try to blind us so that we will not remember whom we have hurt. Satan might also remind us about those who have hurt us in order to distract us. Satan will bring to mind people whom we did not hurt in order to confuse us. Remember, Satan does not want anyone to complete this step. We need to ask God to protect our minds while we complete this step. The Holy Spirit will point out the people whom we have hurt:

> *For we know, brothers loved by God, that he has chosen you, because our gospel came to you not simply with words, but also with power,* **with the Holy Spirit and with deep conviction***.* (1Th.1:4-5 NIV)

When the Holy Spirit convicts us, He pinpoints in a very specific, but gentle, way that we have hurt someone. The Holy Spirit will show us how to make things right. Sometimes, admitting responsibility and saying we are sorry will be enough. Other times, we must replace what we have damaged. God will direct how we should make things right.

FORGIVENESS

When we list the people whom we have hurt, we will be reminded of people who have also hurt us. We must not focus on how they have offended us. Rather, we must forgive them in our hearts and take responsibility for the pain that we have caused them. We must forgive them for the things that they have done to us; otherwise, this will get in the way of making amends. We forgive because God forgave us. The Bible teaches that if we refuse to forgive others, we will not be forgiven by God for our sins:

> And whenever you stand praying, **if you have anything against anyone, forgive him,** that your Father in heaven **may also forgive you your trespasses.** (Mk.11:25 NASB)

We have hurt God many times by our sins. But God still forgave us. God asks us to forgive people for the few times that they have hurt us:

> Be kind to one another, tender-hearted, **forgiving each other, just as God in Christ also has forgiven you**. (Eph.4:32 NASB)

One day, Peter asked Jesus:

> Lord, **how often shall my brother sin against me and I forgive him?** Up to seven times?" Jesus *said to him, "I do not say to you, up to seven times, but up to **seventy times seven.** (Mt.18:21-22 NASB)

God did not mean that we should forgive someone only 77 times. Rather, He meant that we must always forgive. The Bible warns many times that if we do not forgive people, God will not forgive us:

> And whenever you stand praying, if you have anything against anyone, forgive him, that your Father in heaven may also forgive you your trespasses. **But if you do not forgive, neither will your Father in heaven forgive your trespasses**. (Mk.11:25-26 NKJV)

In the book of Luke, God tells us to pray:

> Forgive us our sins, **for** **we also forgive everyone who sins against us**. (Lk.11:4 NIV)

We are forgiven by God as we forgive others:

> Forgive us our sins, **as we have forgiven those who sin against us**. . . . **If you forgive those who sin against you**, your heavenly Father will forgive you. But **if you refuse to forgive others, your Father will not forgive your sins.** (Mt.6:12, 14-15 NLT)

When we show mercy, we forgive people who have hurt us. God only shows mercy to those who show mercy to others:

> *"Blessed are the merciful, **for they shall receive mercy**.* (Mt.5:7 NASB)

Therefore, we must forgive others as God forgave us. Mercy is not optional for a Christian. Since God lives in us, we will be merciful as He is merciful:

> *Therefore be merciful, **just as your Father also is merciful**.*
> (Lk.6:36 NKJV)

THE PRIORITY OF RECONCILIATION

In the North American church culture, many Christians view God's commands as suggestions that we can choose to obey or disobey. In Step 2, we surrendered our lives to God and asked Jesus to live in us and control us. Once we have given control to Jesus, we will begin to think and act like Him. Why did Jesus act the way He did? Jesus said:

> ***"I and My Father are one."*** (Jn.10:30 NKJV)

Jesus is 'one being' with the Father, which means that His will was the same as His Father's will:

> ***For I have come down from heaven**, not to do My own will, but **the will of Him who sent Me**.* (Jn.6:38 NKJV)

Since Jesus is 'one being' with the Father, then both shared the same will. The concept of being one means having one mind and direction:

> *Don't you believe that I am in the Father and the Father is in me? **The words I speak are not my own**, but <u>**my Father who lives in me**</u> <u>**does his**</u> <u>**work**</u> **through me**.* (Jn.14:10 NLT)

When two become one, it not only affects what we do but also how we do it—our attitude:

> *For I did not speak of my own accord, but **the Father who sent me commanded me <u>what</u> to say and <u>how</u> to say it**.* (Jn.12:49 NIV)

The oneness of God made Jesus' will and actions the same as the Father's will, causing Jesus' actions to mirror God's will:

> *The world must learn that **I love the Father** and that **I do exactly what my Father has commanded me**.* (Jn.14:31 NIV)

When our spirits become one with God's Spirit, we share in the oneness of Christ with the Father:

> *"I do not pray for these alone, but also for those who will believe in Me through their word;* **"that they all may be one, <u>as</u> You, Father, are in Me, and I in You;** *that* <u>**they also may be one in Us**</u>, *that the world may believe that You sent Me.* (Jn.17:22-23 NKJV)

The proof of Christ living in us is our obedience to the Father:

> *The* **one who keeps His commandments abides** <u>**in Him, and He in him**</u>. **We know by this that He abides in us, by the Spirit** *whom He has given us.* (1Jn.3:24 NASB)

We do not obey Christ because we have to; rather, we obey Christ because He lives in us. If Christ lives in us, then we will act like Him:

> **For it is God who** <u>**works in you**</u> **to will and to act** *according to his good purpose.* (Php.2:13 NIV)

Christ cannot live in us without controlling us. Since Christ is God and God is a God of peace, then making peace will become important to us:

> *May* **the God of peace. . . equip you** *with everything good for doing his will, and* **may he work in us** *what is pleasing to him, through Jesus Christ, to whom be glory for ever and ever. Amen.* (He.13:20-21 NIV)

We have been changed from being rebellious to being obedient to God by His power which is in us. Hence, disobedience for a Christian is not an option:

> *Go therefore and* **make disciples of all nations**, *baptizing them in the name of the Father and of the Son and of the Holy Spirit, and* **teaching them to obey everything that I have commanded you**. (Mt.28:19-20 NRSV)

A Christian is to be obedient in everything that the Spirit makes known. The Bible tells us of a test to see if our faith is real:

> **Examine yourselves** *to see whether you are in the faith; test yourselves. Do you not realize* **that Christ Jesus is in you— unless, of course, you fail the test?** *And I trust that you will discover that we have not failed the test.* (2Co.13:5-6 NIV)

The test is important. Failing the test proves that Christ does not live in us and we are not saved! What is the test? To find the test we need to go to the beginning of 2 Corinthians:

> *I wrote for this reason:* **to test you** *and to know* **whether you are** <u>**obedient in everything**</u>. (2Co.2:9 NRSV)

Christ came down from heaven and died on the cross to restore God's honor on our behalf. If Christ made peace a priority 2000 years ago, He will make it a priority in our lives today. If Christ lives in us, we will become ministers of peace with our fellow man:

> All this is from God, **who reconciled us to himself through Christ**, and **has given us the ministry of reconciliation**; that is, in Christ God was reconciling the world to himself, not counting their trespasses against them, and **entrusting the message of reconciliation to us.**
> (2Co.5:18-19 NRSV)

Therefore, we must obey God and seek to make things right with people even though it might be difficult. When Zacchaeus became Jesus' follower, he made things right with the people whom he had cheated:

> "Look, Lord! Here and **now I give half my possessions to the poor, and if I have cheated anybody out of anything, I will pay back four times the amount.**"
> (Lk.19:8 NIV)

Jesus said to Zacchaeus:

> "**Today salvation has come to this house**, because he, too, is a son of Abraham."
> (Lk.19:9 NASB)

When Zacchaeus made things right, he showed that he was a follower of Jesus. We must start down the path of peace by making a list of the people whom we have hurt. Therefore, we must first admit to ourselves and God that we are responsible for our sin and the hurt that we have caused others:

> Although he was a Son, he learned obedience through what he suffered; and having been made perfect, **he became the source of eternal salvation for all who obey him.**
> (He.5:8-9 NRSV)

For Further Thought:

We need to make things right with other people because...

1. Why does blaming others keep us from having peace?

2. How can our actions bring shame to others?

3. Why did our sin separate us from God?

4. What is the difference between guilt and shame?

5. What worries you the most about making things right with others?

6. In what four areas are we responsible for our actions?

7. Why must we forgive the people who offended us?

8. What causes us to make things right with other people?

Memory Verse:
Do to others as you would have them do to you.   Luke 6:31

NOTES:

Step 9

Healing the Past

STEP 9 *We will make amends with those whom we have harmed and will attempt to make peace with them, unless by doing so we will cause further harm.*

Humility: The Pathway to Peace

In step 7, we humbled ourselves and asked God to help us. In step 8, we were willing to make amends with the people whom we have hurt. In step 9, we humbly go to these people, admitting that we have hurt them:

> *Do nothing from selfishness or empty conceit,* **but with humility of mind regard one another as more important than yourselves**; *do not merely look out for your own personal interests, but also* **for the interests of others.** (Php.2:3-4 NASB)

We are responsible for the pain that we have caused these people. Therefore, we must humbly go to them and ask for forgiveness. We must lower ourselves and raise them up:

> *Remind them to be subject to rulers and authorities, to obey,* **to be ready for every good work**, *to speak evil of no one,* **to be peaceable**, *gentle,* **showing all humility to all men.** (Ti.3:1-2 NRSV)

We were in the wrong. Therefore, we must be patient and gentle with the people whom we have hurt while they share their side of the story:

> **Be completely humble** *and* **gentle; be patient**, *bearing with one another in love.* (Eph.4:2 NIV)

We should give them time to talk. They may say unkind things to us that will be painful to hear because they are still hurting from our actions. However, we must not defend ourselves or our actions. We must let them talk, because we are responsible for their pain:

> *You must understand this, my beloved: let* **everyone** *be* **quick to listen,**

> *slow to speak, slow to anger;* for your anger does not produce God's righteousness. (Ja.1:19-20 NRSV)

We must not defend ourselves or accuse them of things even if their point of view may not be the same as ours. We must listen, for someone once said, "Pain shared is pain divided." Our listening will aid their healing:

> Finally, all of you, **have unity of spirit**, sympathy, love for one another, a tender heart, and **a humble mind**. Do not repay **evil for evil** or **abuse for abuse**; but, on the contrary, **repay with a blessing**. It is for this that you were called—that you might inherit a blessing. (1Pe.3:8-9 NRSV)

Our example is Jesus. Jesus is God. He became a man because He loved us. Even though we sinned against God, Jesus humbled Himself to save us:

> **Your attitude should be the same as that of Christ Jesus**: Who, being **in very nature God**, did not consider **equality with God** something to be grasped, but **made himself nothing**, taking the **very nature of a servant**, being made in human likeness. And being found in appearance as a man, **he humbled himself and became obedient to death**— even death on a cross! (Php.2:5-8 NIV)

Christ came down from heaven to make peace between us and God. All Christians must humble themselves like Christ. We must humbly go and make peace with the people whom we have hurt. God promises to give us the grace to help us when we go to make things right with others:

> **All** of you, **clothe yourselves with humility toward one another**, for God is opposed to the proud, but **gives grace to the humble**. (1Pe.5:5 NASB)

Therefore, we must humble ourselves and go to the people whom we have hurt. We must let them talk to share their feelings.

LOVE IS NOT OPTIONAL

Our motive to complete step 9 is love. Before we repented and were baptized, we did not care about others. We did not love them:

> For we ourselves were also once foolish, disobedient, deceived, **serving various lusts and pleasures**, **living in malice** and envy, **hateful and hating one another**. (Ti.3:3 NKJV)

We thought only about ourselves. We were selfish because we were controlled by our sinful nature:

> **The acts of the sinful nature** are obvious: sexual immorality, impurity and debauchery; idolatry and witchcraft; **hatred, discord,** jealousy, fits of rage, **selfish ambition**, dissensions, factions and envy; drunkenness, orgies, and the like. I warn you, as I did before, that **those who live like this will not inherit the kingdom of God**. (Ga.5:19-21 NIV)

Once we became Christians, we became different people. We are no longer selfish, but rather we now consider others above ourselves. We love because God, Who is love, lives in our hearts. Because the Holy Spirit controls our hearts, we love the people around us. When our sinful nature controlled our hearts, we did not think about others:

> **The children of God and the children of the devil are revealed in this way:** all who do not do what is right <u>are not from God</u>, nor are **those who <u>do not love</u> their brothers and sisters**. (1Jn.3:10 NRSV)

It is only right to make amends with the people whom we have hurt. If we refuse to make things right, we are not loving these people. Some Christians say, "If you only knew what he did to me, you would not ask me to make amends with him!" However, we gave up the right to hate when we died in our baptism. Bitterness is a form of hatred. If we hate someone, we prove that we are not Christians:

> Whoever says, "I am in the light," while **hating a brother or sister, is still in the darkness.** (1Jn.2:9 NRSV)

If we love someone, we will try to make peace with that person. We do not lose our salvation if we refuse to love. But if we do not love, our actions prove that God does not live in us:

> We know that we **have passed from death to life**, because <u>**we love**</u> **our brothers**. Anyone who <u>**does not love**</u> **remains in death**. Anyone who **hates his brother** is a murderer, and **you know that no murderer has eternal life in him.** (1Jn.3:14-15 NIV)

If we love God, we will start to love all people:

> Those who say, "**I love God**," **and hate their brothers or sisters, are liars**; for those **who do not love a brother or sister whom they have seen**, cannot love God whom they have not seen. The commandment we have from him is this: **those who love God must love their brothers and sisters also**. (1Jn.4:20-21 NRSV)

If we refuse to love the people whom we have hurt, we are not Christians:

> Beloved, let us love one another, for love is from God; and everyone who loves is born of God and knows God. **The one who does not love does not know God, for God is love.** (1Jn.4:7-8 NASB)

Because the Holy Spirit lives in us, we will love the people whom we have hurt. Because we love them, we will make amends with them. Therefore, if we do not make amends with them, we prove that the Holy Spirit does not live in us and we are not Christians.

WE NEED GOD'S LOVE

We must consider the two types of love **in the Bible**: phileo love and agape love. If someone has phileo love, he loves others because they will love him back. If someone has agape love, he will love others even if they continue to hate him. Consider these two types of love:

> **Do to others as you would have them do to you.** "If you love those who love you, what credit is that to you? Even 'sinners' love those who love them. And if you do good to those who are good to you, what credit is that to you? Even 'sinners' do that. And if you lend to those from whom you expect repayment, what credit is that to you? Even 'sinners' lend to 'sinners', expecting to be repaid in full. But **love your enemies, do good to them, and lend to them** without expecting to get anything back. Then your reward will be great, and you will be sons of the Most High, because he is kind to the ungrateful and wicked. Be merciful, just as your Father is merciful. (Lk.6:31-36 NIV)

If a person has only phileo love, he will love his neighbor and hate his enemy. If a person has agape love, he will not only love his neighbor but also love his enemy. Agape love is God's love. Agape love is selfless. If someone has agape love, he loves all people. For Christians, love is not based on feelings. We always show love because the Holy Spirit lives in us and God is love:

> But **the fruit of the Spirit is love**, joy, peace, longsuffering, kindness, goodness, faithfulness, gentleness, self-control. (Ga.5:22-23 NKJV)

When God gave us His Holy Spirit, we received His love—agape love:

> For we know how dearly God loves us, because he has given us **the Holy Spirit to fill our hearts with his love.** (Ro.5:5 NLT; 1Ti.1:14)

The Holy Spirit will increase our love for the people who are not easy to love. Therefore, we will always have enough love to make amends:

> And **may the Lord make your love for one another and for all people grow and overflow**, just as our love for you overflows.
> (1Th.3:12 NLT; 2Th.1:3)

As we make amends, God will increase our love to overflowing. No matter what situation we will face, God will always give us enough love. God will give us more love for the people who are hard to love. Because of God's love, we will want to love the people whom we have hurt:

> We continually remember before our God and Father your work produced by faith, your **labor prompted by love,** and your endurance inspired by hope in our Lord Jesus Christ. (1Th.1:3 NIV)

Because we have God's love, we will want to make things right even though the other people might have hurt us first:

> **In everything** do to others as you would have them do to you; for this is the law and the prophets. (Mt.7:12 NRSV)

When someone hurts us, we want him to say sorry and to make amends. Therefore, we must do the same for the people whom we have hurt. We must ask them to forgive us, and we must try to make things right with them:

> And He said to him, "'**You shall love the Lord your God** with all your heart, and with all your soul, and with all your mind.' "This is the great and foremost commandment. "The second is like it, '**You shall love your neighbor as yourself.**' (Mt.22:37-39 NASB)

Because of our past actions, some people will still hate us after we go to them. We must love these people even if they are unkind to us. God commands us to always love:

> **Owe nothing to anyone—except for your obligation to love one another.** If you love your neighbor, you will fulfill the requirements of God's law. For the commandments say, "You must not commit adultery. You must not murder. You must not steal. You must not covet." These—and other such commandments—are summed up in this one commandment: **"Love your neighbor as yourself."** Love does no wrong to others, so love fulfills the requirements of God's law. (Ro.13:8-10 NLT)

God is love. Because God lives in us, we love others:

> Dear friends, **let us love one another, for love comes from God.** Everyone who loves has been born of God and knows God. Whoever does not love does not know God, because **God is love.** (1Jn.4:7-8 NIV)

We don't make amends because we have to. Rather, we make amends because we truly love the people whom we have hurt. We love because God lives in us. Because God lives in us, love will be our motive in all things:

> **Do everything in love.** (1Co.16:14 NIV)

We cannot love other people by our own strength. Remember that God gave us His Holy Spirit. Therefore, we will love:

> For God has not given us **a spirit** of fear, but **of power and of love** and of a sound mind. (2Ti 1:7 NKJV)

PREPARING HURTING HEARTS FOR AMENDS

When we make amends, some people might get angry. However, this possibility should not stop us. Instead, we must pray before we try to make amends. We must ask God to go before us and to give the person grace. Grace is needed for the person to accept our apology and forgive us:

> **Don't worry about anything; instead, pray about everything.** Tell God what you need, and thank him for all he has done. **Then you will experience God's peace, which exceeds anything we can understand.** His peace will guard your hearts and minds as you live in Christ Jesus. (Php.4:6-7 NLT)

When we make amends with someone, Satan will try to stop us. He will try to make the person angry with us. Satan does not want the person or us to have peace. Satan's mission is **threefold:**

> The thief comes only **to steal** and **kill** and **destroy.** (Jn.10:10 NASB)

Because one of Satan's prime goals is to steal our peace, we must deal with Satan's power over people before we go to make amends:

> I will rescue you from your own people and from the Gentiles. I am sending you to them to **open their eyes and turn them from darkness to light, and from the power of Satan** to God, so that they may receive forgiveness of sins and a place among those who are sanctified by faith in me.' (Ac.26:17-18 NIV)

When we speak to people, Satan will put thoughts into their minds. He wants to cause doubt and twist what we say:

> **You are from your father the devil,** and you choose to do your father's

> desires. He was a murderer from the beginning and does not stand in the truth, because there is no truth in him. **When he lies, he speaks according to his own nature, for he is a liar and the father of lies.**
>
> (Jn.8:44 NRSV)

Our sincere apology can appear shallow and hollow as Satan manipulates the minds of those whom we have hurt. Satan controls non-Christians:

> We know that we are children of God and **that the world around us is under the control of the evil one.** (1Jn.5:19 NLT)

Since Satan controls unbelievers, we must deal with Satan before we make amends:

> Put on the full armor of God, so that you **will be able to stand firm against the schemes of the devil**. For our struggle **is not against flesh and blood**, but against the **rulers**, against the **powers**, against the **world forces of this darkness**, against the **spiritual forces of wickedness** in the heavenly places. (Eph.6:11-12 NASB)

When a person reacts badly, he is not really reacting to us. Rather, he is controlled by Satan. However, Jesus gave us power over Satan and his demons. With Jesus' power, we can command Satan and his demons to be bound from interfering. In this way, Satan will not be able to influence the person:

> Assuredly, I say to you, **whatever you bind on earth will be bound in heaven**, and whatever **you loose on earth will be loosed in heaven**.
>
> (Mt.18:18 NKJV)

However, even after we deal with Satan, the person might still have bad feelings toward us from bitterness. If the person is not a Christian, he does not have the Holy Spirit or the love of God within him. That means that he is still controlled by his sinful nature, making forgiveness unnatural for him. Therefore, we must do two things. First, we must command Satan and his demons to be bound from influencing the person. Second, we must command release of the person's heart from bitterness so that the Holy Spirit can give the person a love to forgive. After we have dealt with Satan's power, then we can go and make amends with the hurt person:

> For when a strong man like Satan is fully armed and guards his palace, **his possessions are safe**—until someone even stronger attacks and **overpowers him**, strips him of his weapons, and **carries off his belongings**. (Lk.11:21-22 NLT)

Jesus gave us authority over Satan's realm. Therefore, we must use God's power to counter the actions of Satan.

LOVING ENOUGH NOT TO MAKE AMENDS

We must always make amends except when to do so would injure the wronged person or others. Because we love this person, we will not try to make amends with him if it will cause greater pain:

> **Love does no wrong to a neighbor.** (Ro.13:10 NASB)

We make amends because we want peace with others. However, we must care more about the person than our peace:

> **Do nothing from selfish ambition or conceit, but in humility** regard others as better than yourselves. Let each of you look not to your own interests, but **to the interests of others**. (Php.2:3-4 NRSV)

Before we make amends, we must pray. The Holy Spirit will tell us whether or not we should make amends. Sometimes, He will tell us to not make amends. In these cases, we must trust that God will give us peace. For we were willing to make amends but were unable:

> **We who are strong ought to bear with the failings of the weak** and not to please ourselves. **Each of us should please his neighbor for his good**, to build him up. (Ro.15:1-3 NIV)

Sometimes, the timing is wrong. The person may be having other problems which make him unable to deal with the hurt from the past. Therefore, we should wait to make amends with him until the Holy Spirit tells us to go. The other person is more important than our peace:

> Do not repay anyone evil for evil. **Be careful to do what is right in the eyes of everybody.** If it is possible, **as far as it depends on you**, live at peace with everyone. (Ro.12:17-18 NIV)

Sometimes, we would hurt someone more if we made amends. For example, if a woman had a secret affair with a man, she should not make amends with the man's wife after she becomes a Christian. If she does, she will destroy his marriage. A Christian should never make amends if it causes further pain:

> The commandments, "Do not commit adultery," "Do not murder," "Do not steal," "Do not covet," and whatever other commandment there may be, are summed up in this one rule: **"Love your neighbor as yourself."** Love

does no harm to its neighbor. *Therefore love is the fulfillment of the law.*
(Ro.13:9-10 NIV)

Sometimes the making of amends will be like opening an old wound. We must love others more than we love ourselves. Therefore, we must care more about their feelings than about our need for peace:

*Let each of you look out not only for his own interests, but **also for the interests of others.*** (Php.2:4 NKJV)

In some cases, a Christian can make amends through another person. For example, a person may have hurt someone's marriage. Although he cannot make amends with the couple whom he has hurt without causing further pain, he can help a different couple that has marriage problems. He could pay for this couple's counseling in place of personally making amends with the couple whom he has hurt. In other cases, the best way to make amends is to change the way we act. We must talk with God as to what is the best way to make amends. We must ask God for wisdom. We must never cause the people more pain when we make amends:

Love is patient; love is kind*; love is not envious or boastful or arrogant or rude.* ***It does not insist on its own way****; it is not irritable or resentful; it does not rejoice in wrongdoing, but rejoices in the truth.* ***It bears all things****, believes all things, hopes all things, endures all things.* ***Love never ends.***
(1Co.13:4-8 NIV)

When we make amends, we should set a time to meet with the person. When we do, we should tell the person that God requires us to ask for forgiveness. However, some people might have moved far away. Therefore, we cannot talk face to face with them. In these cases, we could send them a letter or phone them. Other times, a person might refuse to talk or meet with us. We must try to make amends with everyone whom we have hurt. There will be times when we just can't make amends. The Bible teaches us:

If it is possible, so far as it depends on you*, live peaceably with all.*
(Ro.12:18 NRSV)

We cannot control other people's actions. We can only control our own actions and reactions to them. Therefore, before we make amends, we must pray and listen to the Holy Spirit. He will tell us when and how we should make amends.

DISCERNING AMENDS

Some amends will be difficult to make. Therefore, we must listen to the Holy Spirit while we study the Bible. Then, we will know how we can make amends correctly. Take divorce for an example. If you divorced your husband or wife, you might struggle to make amends with him or her. The Bible gives you two options:

> But to the married I give instructions, not I, but the Lord, that the wife should not leave her husband (but if she does leave, **she must remain unmarried, or else be reconciled to her husband**), and that the husband should not divorce his wife. (1Co.7:10-11 NASB)

As a Christian, either you make peace and return to your spouse, or you make peace and remain unmarried. Regardless of the end result, God wants you to have peace with your former husband or wife. However, because of the past, your husband or wife might not want to meet with you. Sometimes there is a court order preventing you from meeting with your ex-spouse. Therefore, you cannot make peace with him/her directly. If your former husband or wife is not a Christian and does not want to get back together with you, you must let him or her go:

> But if the unbeliever leaves, <u>**let him do so**</u>. **A believing man or woman is <u>not bound</u> in such circumstances;** God has called us to l<u>ive in peace</u>. (1Co.7:15 NIV)

You are **not bound** to keep seeking peace with your former spouse if he/she does not want to be reunited. However, in this case you must remain at peace and unmarried. The unwillingness of a spouse to be reunited does not entitle a person to marry someone else. For in the context of this passage, the Scripture concludes this discussion with a woman being bound to a husband till death:

> **A woman <u>is bound</u> to her husband as long as he lives. But if her husband dies,** she is free to marry anyone she wishes, but he must belong to the Lord. (1Co.7:39 NIV)

This Scripture is clear. If you are divorced, you are not free to remarry:

> For example, a man who **divorces his wife and marries someone else commits adultery.** And anyone **who marries a woman divorced from her husband commits adultery.** (Lk.16:18 NLT)

The person who divorces his spouse on Biblical grounds is not free to remarry until his spouse dies. Biblically, he is considered an adulterer if he remarries. According to God, a marriage covenant is between one man and one woman for life. In other words, you are married to your husband or wife until he or she dies. In the Old Testament, divorce did not dissolve a marriage covenant:

> You ask, "Why?" It is because the LORD is acting as the witness between you and the wife of your youth, because **you have broken faith with her**, though **she <u>is your partner</u>, the wife of your <u>marriage covenant</u>**. Has not the LORD made them one? In flesh and spirit they are his. And why one? Because he was seeking godly offspring. So guard yourself in your spirit, and **do not break faith with the wife** of your youth. "**I hate divorce**," says the LORD God of Israel. (Mal.2:14-16 NIV)

God still considers the wife you married in your youth your marriage partner, even if divorced. Hence, you are still in a marriage covenant after a divorce. In the Old Testament, God commanded that an adulterer be stoned, which ended the marriage covenant through death. In the New Covenant, God allows divorce to separate the faithful spouse from the sexually unfaithful spouse:

> And I say to you, whoever divorces his wife, **except for sexual immorality**, and marries another, commits adultery; and whoever marries her who is divorced commits adultery." (Mt 19:9 NKJV; Mt.5:32)

God only allows divorce because of sexual immorality. If you remarry after divorcing your unfaithful spouse, God calls your second marriage adultery:

> Whoever divorces his wife **and marries another commits adultery** against her. And if a woman divorces her husband **and marries another, she commits adultery**. (Mk.10:11-12 NKJV)

A Christian who remarries after divorcing his spouse for sexual unfaithfulness is an adulterer. Adulterers do not go to heaven when they die:

> **Do you not know that the wicked will not inherit the kingdom of God?** Do not be deceived: **Neither** the sexually immoral nor idolaters nor **adulterers** nor male prostitutes nor homosexual offenders nor thieves nor the greedy nor drunkards nor slanderers nor swindlers **will inherit the kingdom of God.** (1Co.6:9-10 NIV)

Maybe you have a court order to stay away from your husband or wife. In this case, leave him or her alone and live your life for God. Your husband or wife may hear that you have changed and that you are a different person. This may open the door for reuniting:

> *The sins of some men are quite evident, going before them to judgment; for others, their sins follow after.* **Likewise also, deeds that are good are quite evident, and those which are otherwise cannot be concealed.**
> (1Ti.5:24-25 NASB)

Do not force your ex-husband or ex-wife to meet with you. If you do, you will only cause more hurt. Give your 'ex' time. Make it known that you want to get back together with him/her through your friends. You must wait for him/her to make the first move. If your 'ex' is already remarried, then there is nothing that can be done to reunite the marriage. However, asking forgiveness to establish peace must still be pursued, unless it will cause more pain. Therefore, if needed, God wants us to make peace with our former spouse.

In conclusion, we must try to make amends with the people whom we have hurt. Sometimes it will not be possible because of death or distance. Other times our attempt to make peace will only cause more pain. For these situations, an alternative way to make amends should be sought. We must strive to be at peace with everyone.

For Further Thought:

We make amends because...

1. How do you feel about making amends?

2. Why must we be humble when we make amends?

3. Why must a Christian make amends?

4. Why do we need God's love before we can make amends?

5. Why do we need to deal with Satan before we make amends?

6. Why will we not make amends with certain people whom we have hurt?

7. What are some ways that we can make alternative amends?

8. What are our options if we are divorced?

Memory Verse:
If it is possible, as far as it depends on you, live at peace with everyone.
Romans 12:18

NOTES:

Step 10

Growing to Maturity

Step 10 *We will continue to assess our attitudes, behavior, and character, instantly confessing any sin and daily relying on God to transform us into Christ's likeness.*

We Must Continue

One day, a person had a horrible earache. He went to the doctor, and the doctor gave him medicine for 10 days. On day 5, the person felt better, and he stopped taking the medicine. However, a few days later, his earache came back because he stopped taking his medication. In the same way, we cannot stop following the Biblical truths in steps 4-9; or we will return to past sins. Christians must keep following God's teachings as found in the Scriptures:

> *Once you were alienated from God and were enemies in your minds because of your evil behavior. But **now he has reconciled you** by Christ's physical body through death to present you holy in his sight, without blemish and free from accusation—**<u>if you continue</u> in your faith, established and firm, <u>not moved</u>** from the hope held out in the gospel.* (Co.1:21-23 NIV)

God has promised to give us the strength not to sin when we are tempted. We must keep asking Him each day for that strength. We came to Christ believing that He would save us from the penalty for our sin. Now we must continue to ask God to save us from our acts of sin:

> *And now, **just as you accepted Christ Jesus** as your Lord, **you must continue to follow him**. Let your roots grow down into him, and let your lives be built on him.* (Co.2:6-7 NLT)

Humbly we came to Christ and asked Him to change us. We do not depend on ourselves to make right choices. God requires that we ask Him in order to remind ourselves that we can only stop sinning with His help. We rely on God. God promises that He will give us the strength to live each day in holiness:

> *And we have confidence in the Lord concerning you, **that you are doing and will go on doing the things that we command.***
> (2Th.3:4 NRSV)

God enables us to obey. He changes us by living in us, and giving us the power to live to please Him:

> *Therefore, my beloved, **as you have always obeyed**, not as in my presence only, but now much more in my absence, **work out your own salvation** with fear and trembling; **for it is <u>God who works in you</u>** both **to will and to do** for His good pleasure.* (Php.2:12-13 NKJV)

God will help by giving us the strength to make right choices. We will never be perfect, but we must always aim to be perfect:

> *We are glad whenever we are weak but you are strong; and **our prayer is for your perfection... Aim for perfection.*** (2Co.13:9, 11 NIV)

If we do not seek to be perfect, we will return to our past sins. For example, when a man canoes up a river, he is either paddling up the river or drifting back down the river from where he came. Christians must always go against the flow of sin by growing in holiness:

> *Do you not know that those who run in a race all run, but only one receives the prize? **Run in such a way that you may win**. Everyone who competes in the games **exercises self-control in all things**. They then do it to receive a perishable wreath, but we an imperishable. Therefore I run in such a way, as not without aim; I box in such a way, as not beating the air; but **I discipline my body and make it my slave, so that, after I have preached to others, I myself will not be disqualified**.*
> (1Co.9:24-27 NASB)

We will never be completely perfect, but God will keep changing us. Christ's death forgives us when we sin, but His life in us makes us more like Him:

> *For by that one offering **he forever <u>made perfect</u>** those **who <u>are being made</u>** holy.* (He.10:14 NLT)

We can only be sure that God lives in us if our lives keep changing to become more like Him. God calls us to forget our past sins because they are forgiven through Christ's death. When we agree with God that we have sinned, He will also take away our desire to sin. Therefore, we will be forgiven for our sins done in the past, but we must ask God for the strength not to sin today.

THE SIN THAT DOES NOT LEAD TO DEATH

The Scriptures teach that Christians have no excuse to keep on doing the same sins. However, 1 John tells of two types of sins:

> If anyone sees his brother commit **a sin that does not lead to death**, he should pray and God will give him life. I refer to those **whose sin does not lead to death**. There is **a sin that leads to death**. I am not saying that he should pray about that. All wrongdoing is sin, and **there is sin that does not lead to death**. (1Jn.5:16-17 NIV)

Christians sometimes do the type of sin that does not lead to death. When God shows them this sin, they agree with God that the act is sin. Jesus then forgives them, and God gives them the grace to stop doing the sin. Grace gives Christians strength so that they will not keep doing the same sin:

> For we do not have a High Priest who cannot sympathize with our weaknesses, but **was in all points tempted as we are**, **yet without sin**. Let us therefore come boldly to the throne of grace, that we may **obtain mercy** and **find grace to help in time of need**. (He.4:15-16 NKJV)

Let us look at justice, mercy, and grace. **Justice** gives us what we deserve (hell). **Mercy** does not give us what we deserve (hell). **Grace,** however, gives us what we do not deserve (God's help and eternal life in heaven). Grace empowers us to make right choices:

> For **the grace of God** that brings salvation has appeared to all men. **It** teaches us to **say "No" to ungodliness and worldly passions**, and **to live self-controlled, upright and godly** lives **in this present age**. (Ti.2:11-12 NIV)

Even though Christians may discover sin in their lives, God's grace helps us not to continue in that sin:

> My dear children, **I write this to you so that you will not sin**. But **if anybody does sin,** we have one who speaks to the Father in our defense—Jesus Christ, the Righteous One. (1Jn.2:1 NIV)

In the normal Christian life, a person does not keep on doing the same sins. God will not forgive people if they continually choose to do the same sins over and over. In the Old Testament, God only forgave Israel when they sinned in ignorance—not on purpose:

> "'If the whole Israelite **community sins unintentionally** and does what is forbidden in any of the LORD's commands, even though the community is unaware of the matter, they are guilty. **When they become aware of the**

> **sin they committed,** the assembly must bring a young bull as a sin offering and present it before the Tent of Meeting. (Le 4:13-14 NIV)

The Holy Spirit will point out sin to Christians. We do not know that certain things are sin until the Holy Spirit speaks to our hearts. But when the Holy Spirit tells us that they are sin, we will feel guilt if we keep doing them. We will only feel guilt about things that we know are sin:

> "If you were blind, you wouldn't be guilty," Jesus replied. "But you remain guilty **because you claim you can see.**" (Jn.9:41 NLT)

The Holy Spirit is the One Who shows a person his sin. The person must then tell God he is sorry and ask for forgiveness. Our ability to feel guilt is God's way to warn us that He is not pleased and that we must stop:

> If I had not come and spoken to them, **they would not be guilty of sin.** Now, however, **they have no excuse for their sin.** (Jn.15:22 NIV)

Jesus spoke to the Pharisees about their sin. Once they knew their sin, they could no longer tell God that they did not know. Before Paul became a Christian, he sinned without knowing it. Paul thought that he was helping God by hurting Christians:

> Although I was formerly a blasphemer, a persecutor, and an insolent man; but **I obtained mercy because I did it ignorantly in unbelief.**
> (1Ti.1:13 NKJV; note Jn.16:2,3)

Because Paul sinned in ignorance, he did the sin that does not lead to death. He thought he was pleasing God when he did those horrible things. God forgave him when he believed in Jesus and asked to be forgiven. Christians will do things that are wrong because they do not know that those actions go against God's commands. Therefore, Christians will not go to hell for these types of sin. Christians sin without knowing that their actions are wrong. Once they know, they ask God to forgive them for their sin and to help them not to do it again.

CHRISTIANS ARE BLAMELESS

Christians will never be perfect, but they must be without blame. The Bible defines blameless:

> Who can discern his errors? Forgive my hidden faults. **Keep your servant also from willful sins**; may they not rule over me. **Then will I be blameless**, innocent of great transgression. (Ps.19:12-13 NIV)

A blameless person never sins on purpose, and he has dealt with all of the sins that he knows. However, he is not perfect or sinless. There are still sins in his life, but he is not aware of them. A blameless person does not feel guilt because he does not know of any sins in his life which need to be dealt with:

> **My conscience is clear, but that doesn't prove I'm right**. *It is the Lord himself who will examine me and decide.* (1Co.4:4 NLT)

Christians will never be perfect, but the Bible tells us to be blameless:

> *Therefore, beloved, since you look for these things,* **be diligent to be found by Him** *in peace,* **spotless <u>and blameless</u>**.
> (2Pe 3:14 NASB; note Eph.5:27)

The Holy Spirit will keep pointing out our sins. When we confess these sins (tell God we have sinned), God gives us mercy (forgives us) and grace (strength to stop sinning). Mercy is given after we have sinned, while grace is given to keep us from doing the same sin again. We stay blameless when we admit to God that we have sinned and humbly ask Him for mercy and grace:

> *And this I pray,* **that your love may abound still more and more in real knowledge and all discernment**, *so that you may approve the things that are excellent,* **in order to be sincere <u>and blameless</u>** *until the day of Christ.* (Php.2:9-10 NASB)

As we learn more about God, we become more aware of sin. We also learn about God's strength within us. Through God, we can be free from guilt, for He forgives us and helps us not to sin when we are tempted:

> *And* **may <u>he</u> so strengthen** *your hearts* **in holiness that you <u>may be</u> <u>blameless</u> before our God** *and Father at the coming of our Lord Jesus with all his saints.* (1Th.3:13 NRSV)

Jesus, Who lives in us, promises to keep us blameless until we die:

> *You are not lacking in any spiritual gift as you wait for the revealing of our Lord Jesus Christ.* **<u>He will</u>** *also* **<u>strengthen you to the end</u>**, *so* **that you may <u>be blameless</u>** *on the day of our Lord Jesus Christ.* (1Co.1:7-8 NRSV)

We do not keep ourselves blameless. God keeps us blameless:

> *Now* **<u>may the God</u>** *of peace* **make you holy in every way**, *and may* **your whole <u>spirit</u> and <u>soul</u> and <u>body</u> be <u>kept blameless</u>** *until our Lord Jesus Christ comes again.* **<u>God will</u> make this happen**, *for he who calls you is faithful.* (1Th.5:23-24 NLT)

Because God lives within us, we will sin less and less. Christ will give us strength to stop sinning. Paul said that he and his whole missionary team were blameless:

> *You are witnesses, and so is God, **of how holy, righteous and blameless** we were among you who believed.* (1Th.2:10 NIV)

Therefore, we can be sure that we will stop doing the sins that we know. For, when the Spirit shows us sin, He gives us the strength to stop.

THE SIN THAT LEADS TO DEATH

When Christians sin without knowing their actions are wrong, they do the sin that **does <u>not</u> lead to death**. A person does the sin that **leads to death** by knowing that he is sinning but not caring that he has sinned:

> *If anyone sees his brother committing a sin not leading to death, he shall ask and God will for him give life to those who commit sin not leading to death. **There is a sin <u>leading to death</u>**; I do not say that he should make request for this.* (1Jn.5:16 NASB)

The difference between the two types of sin is attitude. The sin that does not lead to death is done by not knowing (ignorance), but the sin that leads to death is done by not caring (apathy). In the Old Testament, God did not forgive His people if they did not care about their sins:

> *But **anyone who <u>sins defiantly</u>**, whether native-born or alien, **blasphemes the LORD**, and that person must be cut off from his people. Because **he has despised the LORD's word** and broken his commands, that person must surely be cut off; **his guilt remains on him**.* (Nu.15:30-31 NIV)

Not all people who call themselves Christian are really Christian. Some people go to church, but they choose to continue doing things they know are sin. This attitude toward sin leads to death. Since they do not care about their sin, God will not forgive them, and they will go to hell:

> *Dear friends, **if we <u>deliberately continue</u> sinning <u>after</u>** we have received knowledge of the truth, **there is no longer any sacrifice that will cover these sins**. There is only the terrible expectation of God's judgment and **the raging fire that will consume his enemies**.* (He.10:26-27 NLT)

God will send a churchgoer to hell if he does not stop doing the sins that he is aware of. After death, God will judge us on what we have done:

> *And as **it is appointed for men to die once**, but after this **the judgment**.* (He.9:27-28 NKJV)

The churchgoer who doesn't care and keeps sinning will suffer in hell:

> But as for the cowardly, the faithless, the polluted, the murderers, the fornicators, the sorcerers, the idolaters, and all liars, **their place will be in the lake that burns with fire** and sulfur, which is **the second death**.
> (Re.21:8 NRSV)

A main part of Christianity is repentance, turning away from those things that we know are sin:

> Therefore **let us leave the elementary teachings about Christ** and go on to maturity, **not laying again the foundation of repentance from acts that lead to death**, and of faith in God, instruction about baptisms, the laying on of hands, the resurrection of the dead, and eternal judgment.
> (He.6:1-2 NIV)

Christ died to forgive us our sin. He rose from the dead to take away our desire to do those things that we know are sin:

> Just think how much more the blood of Christ will **purify our consciences from sinful deeds** so that we can worship the living God.
> (He.9:14 NLT)

If we are born again by the Spirit, we will not keep doing those things that we know are sin:

> **No-one who is born of God will continue to sin**, because God's seed remains in him; **he cannot go on sinning**, because he has been born of God.
> (1Jn3:9 NIV)

If God's Spirit lives in us, He will change us. Our hearts control us, but what controls our hearts? A person is either controlled by his longing to sin or by the Holy Spirit:

> That's why **those who are still under the control of their sinful nature** can never please God. But **you** are **not controlled by your sinful nature**. **You** are **controlled by the Spirit** if you have the Spirit of God living in you. (And remember that **those who do not have the Spirit of Christ living in them do not belong to him at all**.)
> (Ro.8:8-9 NLT)

To keep on doing the things that we know are wrong proves that the Holy Spirit does not live in us. If the Holy Spirit does not live in us, we do not belong to Christ. On the other hand, if the Holy Spirit does live in our hearts, then we will **not** keep on sinning:

> For **if you live according to the sinful nature, you will die**; but **if by the Spirit you put to death the misdeeds of the body, you will live**.

(Ro.8:13 NIV)

The Holy Spirit empowers us to stop sinning:

> So I say, **live by the Spirit, and you will not gratify the desires of the sinful nature.** (Ga.5:16 NIV)

The Holy Spirit gives Christians the desire to live for God by giving them a new nature. Christians have God's divine nature. This nature has a new personality with a desire to please God:

> **His divine power has given us everything needed for life and godliness,** through the knowledge of him who called us by his own glory and goodness. Thus he has given us, through these things, his precious and very great promises, so that through them you may escape from the corruption that is in the world because of lust, and **may become participants of the divine nature.** (2Pe.1:3-4 NRSV)

Since Christians have the Holy Spirit, they live to please God. If we keep living for our sinful nature, we prove that we do not have God's divine nature. A person can only have one nature within him at a time:

> Do not be deceived: God cannot be mocked. A man reaps what he sows. <u>**The one**</u> who sows to please his <u>**sinful nature**</u>, <u>**from that nature**</u> will reap destruction; <u>**the one**</u> who sows **to please the** <u>**Spirit**</u>, <u>**from the Spirit will reap eternal life.**</u> (Ga.6:7-8 NIV)

Are you living to please God, or are you living to please yourself? Look at the list below and then look at your own life:

> **When you follow the desires of your sinful nature**, the results are very clear: sexual immorality, impurity, lustful pleasures, idolatry, sorcery, hostility, quarreling, jealousy, outbursts of anger, selfish ambition, dissension, division, envy, drunkenness, wild parties, and other sins like these. Let me tell you again, as I have before, **that anyone living that sort of life will not inherit the Kingdom of God.** (Ga.5:19-21 NLT)

The Bible states that these actions are sin. We may have done some of these things at one time, but we will stop doing these things if we are Christians:

> **Do you not know that <u>wrongdoers will not</u> inherit the kingdom of God?** Do not be deceived! Fornicators, idolaters, adulterers, male prostitutes, sodomites, thieves, the greedy, drunkards, revilers, robbers—**<u>none of these</u> will inherit the kingdom of God**. And this is what some
>
> of you **used to be**. But you **were** washed, you **were** sanctified, you **were** justified in the name of the Lord Jesus Christ and in the Spirit of our God.

(1Co.6:9-11 NRSV)

Christians will be changed by the Spirit of God. Therefore, if churchgoers keep living to please their sinful desires, they are doing the acts that lead to death. Even if they are trying to appease God by some religious ritual, they will face the raging fires of hell. Christians must turn from their sin and start to live to please God:

> But **God's firm foundation stands**, bearing this inscription: "The Lord knows those who are his," and, "**Let everyone who calls on the name of the Lord <u>turn away from wickedness</u>**." (2Ti 2:19 NRSV)

BLASPHEMY OF THE HOLY SPIRIT

The Bible teaches that the only sin not forgiven is blasphemy against the Holy Spirit. The Old Testament describes blasphemy of God:

> But **anyone <u>who sins defiantly</u>**, whether native-born or alien, **<u>blasphemes the LORD</u>**, and that person must be cut off from his people. Because **he has despised the LORD's word** and broken his commands, that person must surely be cut off; **his guilt remains on him**.
> (Nu.15:30-31 NIV)

If one of God's people keeps choosing to sin on purpose, he has blasphemed God. The New Testament teaches us that we can blaspheme God's Spirit as well:

> I tell you the truth, all sin and blasphemy can be forgiven, but **anyone who blasphemes the Holy Spirit will never be forgiven**. This is a sin with **eternal consequences**. (Mk.3:28-29 NLT)

All sins can be forgiven except blasphemy of the Holy Spirit. It is the only sin which is eternal. To keep sinning after we know the truth is unforgivable:

> If we **<u>deliberately</u> keep on sinning** after we have received the knowledge of the truth, **<u>no sacrifice</u> for sins is left**, but **only a fearful expectation of judgment and of raging fire** that will consume the enemies of God.
> (He.10:26-27 NIV)

If we keep sinning on purpose, no sacrifice for this sin is left because we have trashed God's name. The writer of the book of Hebrews says that to keep sinning on purpose insults the Holy Spirit:

> Anyone who rejected the law of Moses died without mercy on the testimony of two or three witnesses. How much more severely do you think a man

> deserves to be punished **who has trampled the Son of God under foot**, who has treated as an unholy thing the blood of the covenant that sanctified him, and **who has insulted the Spirit of grace?**
> (He.10:28-29 NIV)

The Greek word "blasphemos" (translated "blasphemy") is made from two Greek words: "blato" meaning "to damage" or "to hurt" and "pheme" meaning "reputation, what people think of someone." We must understand that we can hurt a person's reputation by words as well as by actions. The Bible teaches that the Jews blasphemed God by how they lived:

> You who make your boast in the law, do you dishonor God through breaking the law? For **the name of God is blasphemed among the Gentiles because of you.** (Ro.2:17-24 NKJV)

Since God lives in Christians, Christ's name is connected with our sin if we keep on sinning. We hurt the Spirit and shame Christ by continuing to sin:

> For in the case of **those who have once been enlightened** and have tasted of the heavenly gift and **have been made partakers of the Holy Spirit**, and have tasted the good word of God and the powers of the age to come, and then <u>have fallen away</u>, **it is impossible to renew them again to repentance**, since they again crucify to themselves **the Son of God and put Him to open shame**. (He.6:4-6 NASB)

When a churchgoer continues to sin, he is in worse shape than before he said that he believed. For he knows the truth but rejects it:

> **The master of that servant** will come on a day when he does not expect him and at an hour he is not aware of. **He will cut him to pieces and assign him <u>a place with the unbelievers</u>**. That servant **who knows his master's will and** does not get ready or **does not do what his master wants will be beaten with many blows**. (Lk.12:46-47 NIV)

Our knowledge of God makes us responsible to Him. Our continual disobedience is an even greater offense than our not believing in Christ:

> For if, after they have escaped the defilements of the world by the knowledge of the Lord and Savior Jesus Christ, they are again entangled in them and are overcome, **the last state has become <u>worse for them than the first</u>**. For it would be better for them <u>not to have known the way of righteousness</u>, **than having known it, to turn away** from the holy commandment handed on to them. (2Pe.2:20-21 NASB)

A churchgoer who keeps sinning is guilty of turning his back on the Holy

Spirit:

> *For God did not call us to be impure, but to live a holy life.* *Therefore, he who **rejects this instruction** does not reject man but God, who gives you **his Holy Spirit**.*" (1Th.4:7-8 NIV)

Only a person who claims to be a Christian can blaspheme God by the way he lives. This person says that he is a Christian but does not change when the Holy Spirit speaks to him about his sin. When a churchgoer refuses to stop his sin, the church must stop spending time with him:

> *I wrote to you in my epistle not to keep company with sexually immoral people. Yet I certainly did not mean with the sexually immoral people of this world, or with the covetous, or extortioners, or idolaters, since then you would need to go out of the world.* ***But now I have written to you not to keep company <u>with anyone named a brother</u>, who is sexually immoral,*** *or covetous, or an idolater, or a reviler, or a drunkard, or an extortioner—not even to eat with such a person. For what have I to do with judging those also who are outside? Do you not judge those who are inside?* (1Co.5:9-11 NKJV)

Therefore, if we say that we are Christians but keep choosing to sin, we make others think wrongly about Christ and blaspheme the Holy Spirit.

A Time for Examination

Christians must be free from sin. We must ask the Holy Spirit to show us if there are any sins in our lives. We must carefully look at all of our actions to find any sins:

> *Whoever, therefore,* **eats the bread or drinks the cup of the Lord** *in an <u>unworthy manner will be answerable</u> for the body and blood of the Lord.* **Examine yourselves, and only then eat** *of the bread and drink of the cup.* (1Co.11:26-28 NRSV)

The Bible says that we must look for sin in our lives before we eat of the Lord's Supper. If we find any sin, we need to ask God for forgiveness and for cleansing from the desire to do it again. Before the first Lord's Supper, Jesus washed His disciples' feet. Peter would not let Jesus wash his feet:

> *Peter said to Him, "You shall never wash my feet!" Jesus answered him,* ***"If I do not wash you, you have no part with Me."*** (Jn.13:8 NKJV)

To say that someone has no part of Christ is to say that he is not a Christian. Jesus said that He had to wash His disciples' feet. Jesus was not worried about the dirt on their feet. He was talking about the uncleanness of sin that had collected in their hearts:

> Jesus answered, "A person who has had a bath needs only to wash his feet; his whole body is clean. **And you are clean, though <u>not every one of you</u>.**" For **he knew who was going to betray him**, and that was why he said not every one was clean. (Jn.13:10-11 NIV)

Judas' feet were not dirtier than the other disciples. However, Judas' heart was not clean because he told the Jewish leaders that he would help them kill Jesus:

> After this, **Jesus and his disciples** went out into the Judean countryside, where **he spent some time with them, and baptized.** (Jn.3:22 NIV)

Even though Judas was baptized by Jesus, he loved money more than Jesus. After Judas left the meeting, Jesus washed the disciples' feet to clean them from any sin that they had done since their baptism. Before we eat the Lord's Supper, we need to look for any sin in our lives, and we need to ask God to cleanse us from those sins. Jesus said that we should look for sin in our lives before we eat the Lord's Supper. Jesus also taught that we will be blessed if wash each other's feet, an act which is a form of spiritual washing:

> If you know these things, **you are blessed <u>if you do them</u>**. (Jn.13:17 NASB)

Foot washing is a form of cleansing from the sin that the Holy Spirit has pointed out in our lives since the last spiritual washing. God warns us:

> Therefore, whoever eats the bread or drinks the cup of the Lord in an unworthy manner will be guilty of sinning against the body and blood of the Lord. **A man ought to <u>examine himself</u> before he eats of the bread and drinks of the cup.** For all who eat and drink <u>without discerning</u> the body, **eat and drink judgment against themselves**. For this reason many of you **are weak and ill, and some have died**. But **if we judged ourselves**, we would not be judged. (1Co.11:29-31 NRSV)

Jesus came to take away all of our sin. Therefore, we must keep doing the steps found in these studies. When the Holy Spirit points out sin in our lives, He will also give us the strength to overcome our sin.

For Further Thought:

We must keep using the 12 steps to stop our sinning because…

1. When is it time to stop using the 12 steps?

2. Why must we always try to please God?

3. What is different between being perfect and being blameless?

4. What is different between "the sin that does not lead to death" and "the sin that leads to death?"

5. How can someone blaspheme the Holy Spirit?

6. How can we be worse off after we said that we believe in Jesus then before?

7. When does the Bible command us to look for sin in our lives?

8. Why does the Scripture say foot washing is important?

Memory Verse:
No one who lives in him keeps on sinning. No one who continues to sin has either seen him or known him.   1 John 3:6

NOTES:

Step 11

Communion With God

Step 11 *We will constantly pray about all things, study God's Word for His truth, and ask His Spirit to grant us His love, wisdom, holiness, and power.*

Our Spirit

God created everything in the heavens and on the earth. Everything was created by God for His glory. God created us special. We were made in His own likeness:

> *Then God said, "**Let Us make man in Our image**, according to **Our likeness**. . . And God created man in **His own image, in the image of God He created him**.* (Ge.1:26-27 NASB)

God made us like Himself, in three parts. God is one being, existing in the Father, the Son, and the Holy Spirit. Each part of God has His own special abilities:

> *Who have been chosen <u>according</u> to **the foreknowledge of God the Father**, <u>through</u> the **sanctifying work of the <u>Spirit</u>**, <u>for</u> **obedience to Jesus Christ**.* (1Pe.1:2 NIV)

We were made of two things: the dust/dirt of the ground and the breath of God. When these two things were put together by God, they made a third part, a living soul:

> *And the LORD God formed man of **the dust of the ground**, and **breathed into his nostrils** the breath of life; and **man became a living soul**.* (Ge.2:7 KJV)

The dust, soul, and breath stand for our three different parts: body, soul, and spirit:

> *May the God of peace himself sanctify you entirely; and may your **spirit and soul and body** be kept sound and blameless at the coming of our Lord Jesus Christ.* (1Th.5:23-24 NRSV)

Our body was created so that we can connect to the physical world with our five senses: touch, taste, sight, smell, and hearing. Our soul is who we are. Each person is different in nature, in likes and dislikes, and in past experiences. Our soul was created so that we can think (intellect), desire (emotion), and make choices (will). Our spirit was created to know God. Each part of us has unique abilities: the soul cannot feel a chair, and the body cannot think. Our spirit was created to control our soul, and our soul was created to control our body. When God created man, He gave Adam His first command:

> And the LORD God commanded the man, "You are free to eat from any tree in the garden; but **you must not eat** from the tree of the knowledge of good and evil, for **when you eat** of it **you will surely die**."
> (Ge.3:16-17 NIV)

God told Adam that the penalty for breaking His one law was death. When Adam and Eve ate the forbidden fruit, God could have killed mankind that day, but He was merciful. Since the penalty was death and God is just, Adam and Eve had to die in some way that day. They did not die physically because they continued to live and have children. Nor did they die soulically, causing them to be brain dead. Instead, their spirit died that day. No longer could Adam and Eve continue in their relationship with God. When Adam and Eve's spirit died, it died for their children as well:

> For as **in Adam all die**. (1Co.15:22 KJV)

The New Testament teaches that everyone related to Adam has already died in Adam:

> For if **the many died** by the trespass of the **one man**. (Ro 5:15 NKJV)

Everyone born from Adam is born alive in body but dead in spirit. In the Old Testament, God promised Israel that one day He would place a new heart and a new spirit in us:

> **I will give you a new heart and put a new spirit in you**; I will remove from you your heart of stone and give you a heart of flesh. And **I will put my Spirit in you and move you to follow my decrees and be careful to keep my laws.** (Eze.36:26 NIV; Eze.11:19-20)

Our new heart makes it possible for the Holy Spirit to live in us, while our new spirit enables us to have a relationship with God. God kept this promise on Pentecost:

> **By this he meant the Spirit,** whom those who believed in him **were later to receive.** <u>Up to that time</u> **the Spirit had not been given**, since Jesus had not yet been glorified. (Jn.7: 39 NIV)

Jesus had to die and pay the penalty for our sins before the Holy Spirit could live in people. Once Jesus' Spirit comes into our lives, our spirits are given life:

> "I tell you the truth, those who listen to my message and believe in God who sent me **have eternal life**. They will never be condemned for their sins, but **they have already passed from death into life**. (Jn.5:24 NLT)

When our spirits are made alive (born again), they become one with the Holy Spirit, allowing us to have a relationship with God:

> Do you not know that whoever is united to a prostitute becomes one body with her? For it is said, "The two shall be one flesh." But **anyone united to the Lord becomes <u>one spirit with him</u>**. (1Co.6:16-17 NRSV)

Therefore, through Christ, a Christian's spirit is given life and becomes one in spirit with God's Spirit.

TO KNOW GOD'S WORD

In the Bible there are three different types of relationships that people can have with God: an unbelieving relationship, an intermittent relationship, and a believing relationship. An unbelieving relationship is not relationship at all. An intermittent relationship is an Old Testament relationship in which God comes upon a person for a short amount of time. A believing relationship is one in which the person has the Holy Spirit living within him and is one in spirit with God. This is a Christian relationship. Once our spirits are given life, we can experience a personal relationship with God. Some people try to know about God by studying His Word just like they study math or history. But Christians are told that they can personally know God:

> My Father has entrusted everything to me. No one truly knows the Son except the Father, and **no one truly <u>knows the Father</u>** except the Son and **those to whom the Son chooses to reveal him**" (Mt.11:27 NLT)

Jesus came so that all people can have a relationship with God:

> No longer will a man teach his neighbor, or a man his brother, saying, 'Know the Lord,' because **they will <u>all know me</u>**, from **the least** of them to **the greatest**. (He.8:11 NIV)

If you are a Christian, then you can know God. You can have a personal relationship with Him. This is clearly seen in the two different Greek words for the "Word of God": "logos" and "rhema." The one we know best is "logos," the written Word of God (Bible). Christians can hear God speaking to their hearts through the written Word of God. Many churchgoers read the Bible but cannot understand it. They are like the Ethiopian in the book of Acts:

> Then Philip ran up to the chariot and heard the man reading Isaiah the prophet. **"Do you understand what you are reading?"** Philip asked. **"How can I,"** he said, **"unless someone explains it to me?"** So he invited Philip to come up and sit with him. (Ac.8:30-31 NIV)

The Ethiopian was still dead in his spirit; he was an unbeliever. He needed someone to explain the Bible. Being smart (intellect) does not help us to understand the Bible. Only the Holy Spirit can help us by revealing the true meaning of the Scriptures (intuition):

> **But people who aren't spiritual can't receive these truths** from God's Spirit. It all sounds foolish to them and **they can't understand it**, for **only those who are spiritual can understand what the Spirit means**. (1Co.2:14 NLT)

Once the Ethiopian's spirit was given life through baptism, the Holy Spirit took Philip away. Even though the Ethiopian had just heard about Jesus, being joined with the Spirit of God was all that he needed. The Holy Spirit is all that we need to understand the Scriptures. Many churchgoers are like the disciples who walked with Jesus. Jesus often spoke plainly about His death and the things that were to come, but they could not understand these things. However, after Jesus' resurrection, He gave the disciples the ability to understand the Scriptures:

> Then **he opened their minds to understand the scriptures.** (Lk.24:45 NRSV)

Jesus opened their minds by having the Holy Spirit come upon them:

> So Jesus said to them again, "Peace be with you; as the Father has sent Me, I also send you." And when He had said this, **He breathed on them and said to them, "Receive the Holy Spirit."** (Jn.20:21-22 NASB)

The disciples, before Pentecost, had the same experience as the Old Testament prophets. The Spirit came **upon** them. However, it was only after Pentecost that the disciples' spirits came alive and became one with

God's Spirit. This experience was different. After Pentecost, the Holy Spirit **dwelled within** them with all of His fullness:

> Now when they saw the boldness of Peter and John, and **perceived that they were uneducated and untrained men**, they marveled. And **they realized that they had been with Jesus**. (Ac.4:13 NKJV)

Paul always prayed for those who came to believe through his teaching:

> **I keep asking** that the God of our Lord Jesus Christ, the glorious Father, **may give you the <u>Spirit of wisdom and revelation</u>**, so that you may know him better. (Eph.1:17 NIV; Ja.1:5-6)

Only the Holy Spirit can teach us the true meaning of the Scriptures. We need God to give us wisdom to know how the Bible applies to our lives:

> For this reason, since the day we heard about you, **we have not stopped praying for you and asking God to fill you with the knowledge of his will through all spiritual wisdom and understanding**. (Co.1:9 NIV)

Every Christian can know the truth through the Holy Spirit:

> But you are not like that, for **the Holy One has given you his Spirit, and <u>all of you know the truth</u>**. So I am writing to you not because you don't know the truth but **because <u>you know</u> the difference between truth and lies**. (1Jn. 2:20-21 NLT)

The Holy Spirit's ability to teach Christians is so effective that we do not need human teachers. The Holy Spirit will teach us about all things:

> As for you, the anointing that you received from him abides in you, and so **you do not need anyone to teach you**. But as **his anointing teaches you <u>about all things</u>**, and is true and is not a lie, and just as it has taught you, abide in him. (1Jn.2:27 NRSV; Jn.16:12-13)

If we have the Spirit living in us, then He will teach us all that we need to know:

> I myself am convinced, my brothers, that you yourselves are full of goodness, **<u>complete</u> in knowledge and <u>competent</u> to instruct one another**. (Ro.15:14 NIV)

We are not like God, Who knows everything (omniscience). But God will teach us all that we need to know for every situation, each moment of the day. We need to stop trying to understand by our own abilities and start listening to God about His Scriptures:

> For **in him you have been enriched in every way**—*in all your speaking and* **in all your knowledge**—*because our testimony about Christ was confirmed in you.* (1Co.1:5-6 NIV)

Therefore, understanding the logos/Bible is a gift from the Holy Spirit. The Holy Spirit will open our minds as we study the Scriptures:

> *And we know that* **the Son of God has come and has given us understanding** *so that we may* **know him who is true**. (1Jn.5:20 NRSV)

To Know God's Voice

The second Greek word that is translated "Word of God" is "rhema." This Word of God is spoken into our hearts by the Holy Spirit. Jesus said that He was like a shepherd, and we are like His sheep. In Jesus' day, the shepherd and the sheep had a relationship. The sheep knew the voice of the shepherd and followed him. They obeyed the voice of the shepherd. To follow God, we need to know His voice:

> **The sheep hear his voice, and he calls his own sheep by name** *and leads them out. When he puts forth all his own, he goes ahead of them, and* **the sheep follow him because they know his voice**. (Jn.10:3-4 NASB)

When I first became a Christian, God taught me His truth; but I lacked direction. I tried to serve God by helping my fellow man. However, my actions did not seem to bring anyone closer to God. In order to truly help people, we must work with God, obeying His voice. Many people look at their day or a situation, and then decide what they think is the best thing to do. However, God does not want us to do what we think is best. God wants us to do whatever He asks, when He asks. With God there is only one thing that He asks us to do at a time—His will:

> *For we are God's workmanship, created in Christ Jesus* **to do good works**, *which God* <u>**prepared in advance**</u> **for us to do**. (Eph.2:10 NIV)

The Bible often speaks of people receiving a word from God to do something special. In fact, the Old Testament uses the phrase **"the Word of the Lord"** 224 times—meaning that God told His people what He wanted done. The prophets of the Old Testament heard the voice of God speaking to their hearts:

> *But know this first of all, that no prophecy of Scripture is a matter of one's own interpretation, for no prophecy was ever made by an act of human will, but **men moved by the Holy Spirit spoke from God**.*
> (2Pe.1:20-21 NASB)

God usually speaks to our hearts in a still, quiet voice. All Christians can hear God's voice if they would only stop and listen:

> ***My sheep hear My voice***, *and I know them, and **they follow Me**.*
> (Jn.10:27 NASB)

Thoughts can come from different places. We need to determine whether God was the One Who spoke to us. Our thoughts can come from God, our own minds, or Satan. The Bible teaches that we can tell where our thoughts come from by comparing our thoughts with the written Word of God:

> *For **the word of God is living and active** and sharper than any two-edged sword, and piercing as far as **the division of <u>soul and spirit</u>**, of both joints and marrow, and **able to judge <u>the thoughts and intentions</u> of the heart**.*
> (He.4:12 NASB)

The written Word of God helps us to know if a thought comes from our soul (intellect/mind) or from the Spirit. When a thought comes into our minds, we use the Scriptures to check if the thought was from God. The Holy Spirit will never go against the written Word of God:

> *Learn from us the meaning of the saying, "**Do not go beyond what is written.**" Then you will not take pride in one man over against another.*
> (1Co.4:6 NIV)

When God speaks into our hearts, what He tells us to do will always agree with what is written in the Word of God. If what we hear does not agree with the New Testament, we know that it did not come from God. God gives us two points to focus upon: God's written Word and His spoken Word by the Holy Spirit in our hearts. Trying to walk in obedience to God is like walking in a straight line. If I were to take one marker, say a stop sign, and keep my eye focused on it, I would not walk in a straight line. In fact, I might end up walking in zigzags or even circles around the sign. Similarly, we will walk in circles if we only listen to our hearts. To hear a voice speaking in our hearts is not good enough. To walk a straight line, we need two points to focus upon. If I were to choose that stop sign and a no parking sign some distance away and keep these two signs lined up, I would walk in a straight line. I can either look from the stop sign to the no parking sign or from the no parking sign to the stop sign. Walking with my eye focused on these two points will enable me to walk a straight line. In seeking God's will for our lives, we must keep what God says to our hearts in line with the New Testament. Comparing these two points enables us to walk in God's will. We can either look from what He has said in our hearts (rhema) to His written Word (logos), or from God's written Word to His word spoken in our hearts. Both must line up if we want to live in the center of His will. Without the written Word, we would not be able to decide if it was God Who spoke to us:

> **All Scripture is given by inspiration of God**, and is profitable for doctrine, for reproof, for correction, for instruction in righteousness, that **the man of God may be complete, thoroughly equipped for every good work.** (2Ti.3:16-17 NKJV)

We must compare what we hear in our hearts with the Scriptures. The Bereans understood the importance of checking with the Word of God:

> And the people of Berea were more open-minded than those in Thessalonica, and they listened eagerly to Paul's message. **They searched the Scriptures day after day to see if Paul and Silas were teaching the truth.** (Ac.17:11 NLT)

Everything that comes from God will always agree with the New Testament. God's Spirit, Who spoke through men and wrote the Scriptures, is the same Spirit Who speaks into our hearts. God does not change His mind or His Word:

> **God is not a human being,** that he should lie, or **a mortal, that he should change his mind.** Has he promised, and will he not do it? Has he spoken, and will he not fulfill it? (Nu.23:19 NRSV)

Since God does not change, we know that the Holy Spirit will never tell us to do anything that would go against what Jesus taught. If God has spoken to our hearts, then what has been said will line up with the New Testament. When these two points line up, we must obey, believing that this is God's will for our lives:

> **Everything that does not come from faith is sin.** (Ro.14:23 NIV)

If we do not have faith that God was the One Who spoke to us, than the action could be sin. The New Testament tells us to do many things, but a man can only do one thing at a time. For example: some people might ask me, "Why didn't you visit John since he is very sick?" I respond, "Because God told me to share the Gospel with Sam today." Christians need to carefully hear God's will for their lives by constantly listening to His voice (rhema). I am talking about all of the everyday choices of normal life. For this reason, we must know God in order to know His will. Christians live and act by faith:

> For in the gospel a righteousness from God is revealed, a righteousness that is by faith from first to last, just as it is written: **"The righteous will live by faith."** (Ro.1:17 NIV)

The previous verse states that we will live by faith and not that the righteous receive life by faith. We must walk in the faith that God is the One speaking to us, and we must be obedient to His voice:

> These promote controversies **rather than God's work—which is by faith**. (1Ti.1:4 NIV; 1Th.1:3)

Faith is the check and balance to the Scripture. In faith, we must believe that God has spoken to us:

> We have different gifts, according to the grace given us. If a man's gift is prophesying, **let him use it in proportion to his faith**. (Ro.12:6 NIV)

Without the faith that God has called you, even becoming a pastor or missionary is sin. In this way, God uses faith as the means to lead us:

> We constantly pray for you, that our God may count you worthy of his calling, and that by his power he may fulfill every good purpose of yours and **every act prompted by your faith**." (2Th.1:11 NIV)

If God wants anyone to do something, He will give him the faith to obey His voice. Once we are directed by our faith to step out, we must compare it to the New Testament. If they agree, then we know that our actions are the will of God:

> Trust in the LORD with all your heart, And lean not on your own understanding; **in all your ways acknowledge Him**, And He shall direct your paths. (Pr.3:5-6 NKJV)

Therefore, God wants us to know the Scripture, which is His general will for His children. He also wants us to know His voice so that we can know His will for each moment.

To Know His Power

To know the Word of God and the will of God without the power to act upon it is frustrating. Before Paul was saved and was living by the Law, he knew the Word of God and the will of God. But Paul did not have the power to follow through and obey it:

> I know that **nothing good lives in me**, that is, in my sinful nature. For **I have the desire to do what is good**, but **I cannot carry it out**. For what I do is not the good I want to do; no, **the evil I do not want to do—this I keep on doing**. Now if I do what I do not want to do, it is no longer I who do it, but it is sin living in me that does it. (Ro.7:18-20 NIV)

Before the Holy Spirit lived in Paul, he could not do the will of God. Sin is disobedience to God. Once a person becomes a Christian, God's power will give him the strength to obey Him:

> Anyone who continues to live in him will not sin. But **anyone who keeps on sinning does not know him** or understand who he is. (1Jn.3:6 NLT)

To keep sinning through disobedience after we say that we know Him is to have our actions disagree with our claims:

> **They profess to know God, but they deny him by their actions**. They are detestable, disobedient, unfit for any good work. (Ti.1:16 NRSV)

The Gospel of Jesus Christ has the power to change any life:

> For the message of the cross is foolishness to those who are perishing, but **to us who are being saved it is the power of God**. (1Co.1:18 NKJV)

The apostle Paul writes about the source of God's power:

> I want to know Christ and **the power** of his resurrection. (Php.3:10 NRSV)

Christ died to be our Savior, but He rose from the dead to be our Lord. Christ arose from the dead to live in us and give us the power over sin:

> And **if Christ has not been raised**, our **preaching is useless** and **so is your faith**... And **if Christ has not been raised**, your **faith is futile**; you are **still in your sins**. Then those also who have **fallen asleep in Christ are lost**. (1Co.15:14, 17-18 NIV)

Christ's resurrection from the dead gives Christians power over sin. The apostles knew about Christ as Savior, for the Holy Spirit was with them when they walked with Jesus. After Jesus' death, He would not let them go out into the world and share the Gospel until after Pentecost. Only then were they personally given His power within them:

> *I am sending upon you what my Father promised; so* **stay here in the city until you have been clothed with power** *from on high.*
>
> (Lk.24:49 NRSV)

On the day of Pentecost, the Spirit came to live in them:

> *"I will ask the Father, and He will give you another Helper, that He may be with you forever; that is* **the Spirit of truth**, *whom the world cannot receive, because it does not see Him or know Him, but* **you know Him because He abides with you and will be in you**.   (Jn.14:16-17 NASB)

The power of God is found in us through the Holy Spirit:

> *I pray that out of his glorious riches* **he may strengthen you with power through his Spirit in your inner being**, *so that Christ may dwell in your hearts through faith.*   (Eph.3:16-17 NIV)

All Christians have the power of God within them because the Holy Spirit lives within them:

> *For God did not give us a spirit of cowardice, but rather* **a Spirit of power** *and of love and of self-discipline.*   (2Ti 1:7 NRSV)

There is a great difference between **knowing about** God and **knowing Him** living in us. When He lives in us, He gives power to our lives. God's power changes our lives completely to become more like Jesus:

> *And we pray this in order that you may live a life worthy of the Lord and may* **please him in every way**: *bearing* **fruit in every good work**, *growing in the knowledge of God, being* **strengthened with all power** *according to his glorious might.*   (Co.1:10-11 NIV)

We are not all-powerful but the all-powerful God lives in us. No matter what we might be facing, God can help us:

> *Jesus said to them,* **"With people this is impossible**, *but* **with God all things are possible."**   (Mt 19:26 NASB)

My Christian life is not about me. It is about God's fullness living in and through me:

> *For in Christ* **all the fullness of the Deity lives** *in bodily form, and* **you have been given fullness** *in Christ.*   (Co.2:9-10 NIV)

God lives in me, and by faith I believe that He will change my life:

> **Work hard to show the results of your salvation**, obeying God with deep reverence and fear. For **God is working in you, giving you the desire and the power to do** what pleases him.   (Php.2:12-13 NLT)

We must keep an attitude of humility because He is the One Who works in us. God gives us the will and the power to make right choices:

> May the God of peace... **equip you with everything good for doing his will,** and **may <u>he work</u> in us what is pleasing to him**, through Jesus Christ, to whom be glory for ever and ever. Amen.   (He.13:20-21 NIV)

Once a person has given his life to Christ, Christ will live in him and will keep him from continuing in sin:

> We want to present them to God, **perfect in their relationship to Christ**. That's why I work and struggle so hard, **<u>depending on Christ's</u> mighty power that works within me**.   (Co.1:28-29 NLT)

We will still be tempted by Satan, but the Holy Spirit will give us the power to walk above temptations:

> His divine power has given us **everything needed for life and godliness.**   (2Pe 1:3 NRSV)

The power to become holy is in Christ, Who lives in us through His Holy Spirit. So many Christians only talk about God without knowing Christ's power to change them from within:

> For the kingdom of God **does not consist in words but in power**.   (1Co.4:20 NASB)

We must tell people that the power to change can only be found in God:

> But we have this treasure in clay jars, so that it may be made clear that **this <u>extraordinary power belongs to God</u> and does not come from us.**   (2Co.4:7 NRSV)

We must give God the credit for the change in our lives. Giving God the glory releases God's power throughout our lives:

> Now **to Him <u>who is able to do far more</u> abundantly beyond all that we ask or think, according to the power** that **works within us**, to Him be the glory in the church.   (Eph.3:20 NASB)

Therefore, God has given us the ability to know Him and His will for our lives, and He has given us the power to carry out His will. All the glory belongs to Him.

For Further Thought:

The most important part of Christianity is...

1. What died when Adam and Eve ate the forbidden fruit?

2. How is it possible for all Christians to know God?

3. People's relationship with the Holy Spirit is different in the Old Testament when compared to the New Testament. Why?

4. What is the difference between being complete in knowledge and being all-knowing?

5. How can you be sure if a thought came from God?

6. What does it mean to walk by faith?

7. If Christ was not raised from the dead, we are still in our sin. Why?

8. Without Christ, everyone is powerless to change. How did Christ make a difference?

Memory Verse:
This is how we know we are in him: Whoever claims to live in him must walk as Jesus did.   1John 2:5-6

NOTES:

Step 12

Sharing the Vision

Step 12 *We, having been born again, will in love share His Gospel with others, asking Him to set up divine appointments with those whom He has called.*

You Must be Born Again

Step 12 can only be done by those who have had a spiritual awakening. The Bible calls this being born again:

> Jesus answered and said to him, "Truly, truly, I say to you, **unless one is born again** he **cannot see the kingdom of God.**" (Jn.3:3 NASB)

There is physical birth, and then there is spiritual birth. In the same way that a mother's body controls the time of physical birth, God controls the time of our spiritual birth:

> Yet to all who received him, to those who believed in his name, **he gave the right** to become children of God— children born not of natural descent, nor of human decision or a husband's will, **but born of God**. (Jn.1:12-13 NIV)

Only God's Spirit can give birth to our spirits:

> Jesus replied, "I assure you, no **one can enter the Kingdom of God without being born of water and the Spirit.** Humans can reproduce only human life, but **the Holy Spirit gives birth to spiritual life.** So don't be surprised when I say, '**You must be born again.**' (Jn.3:5-7 NLT)

When the Spirit comes into our lives, we are born again. Our spiritual birth began when someone shared the Gospel with us:

> **For you have been born again**, not of perishable seed, but of imperishable, **through the living and enduring word of God.** (1Pe.1:23 NIV)

Just as a physical mother has labor pains, our spiritual birth starts with hearing the Gospel. We must hear the Gospel **and** turn to God by obeying its truth:

> *He saved us,* **not because of any works of righteousness that we had done,** *but according to his mercy,* **through the <u>water of rebirth</u> and <u>renewal by the Holy Spirit</u>**. *This Spirit he poured out on us richly through Jesus Christ our Savior.* (Ti.3:5-6 NRSV)

Once we believe, our first step of obedience is baptism. Spiritual life is like a journey; every journey starts by taking its first step. Baptism, a washing of rebirth, is the first step in our spiritual journey. Before we can be born again, we need to die to what we were:

> *How shall* **we who died to sin** *still live in it? Or do you not know that all of us who* **have been baptized into Christ Jesus have been baptized into His death?** *Therefore we have been* **buried with Him through baptism into death**, *so that as Christ was raised from the dead through the glory of the Father, so we too might walk in newness of life.*
> (Ro.6:2-4 NASB)

We died in our baptism to sin. Sin lost its power when we gave up our right to chose and made Christ our Lord. Our sinful nature also had to die:

> *In him you were also circumcised,* **in the putting off of the sinful nature**, *not with a circumcision done by the hands of men but with the* **circumcision done by Christ, having been buried with him in baptism** *and raised with him through your faith in the power of God, who raised him from the dead.* (Co.2:11-12 NIV)

Our sinful nature died in our baptism and has been replaced with a divine nature. Finally, we died to the world with its distractions. The world is Satan's system for controlling us:

> *May I never boast of anything except the cross of our Lord Jesus Christ,* **by which the world has been crucified to me, and I to the world.** *For neither circumcision nor uncircumcision is anything; but* **a new creation is everything!** (Ga.6:14-15 NRSV)

Unless people become born again by placing their lives under the control of God, they will keep suffering under Satan's control:

> *We know that* **<u>anyone born of God</u>** *does not continue to sin;* <u>**the one who was born of God keeps him safe**</u>, *and* <u>**the evil one cannot harm him**</u>. *We know that we are children of God, and that* **the whole world <u>is under the control of the evil one</u>**. (1Jn.5:18-19 NIV)

Every person needs to be born again. People in the world and churchgoers both need to hear this message. Many churchgoers have gone to church most of their lives but have never died and been born again. You cannot become a Christian without becoming a new creation:

> So *if* anyone is **in Christ**, there is a **new creation**: <u>everything</u> old has passed away; see, <u>everything</u> has become new! (2Co.5:17 NRSV)

Our new birth changes who we are. We were sinners, but we now are saints by faith. If God promises something and we believe it, then we will receive it. Some people call themselves Christian and yet are still trapped in sin. Christians believe that they have the power to overcome the world by God's presence within them:

> **Loving God means keeping his commandments**, and his commandments are not burdensome. For every child of God **defeats this evil world**, and **we achieve <u>this victory through our faith</u>**. And who can win this battle against the world? **Only those who believe that Jesus is the Son of God.** (1Jn.5:3-5 NLT)

The act of baptism alone does not free us from sin, Satan, and the world. God does it. Our faith is in God that He will do as He promised. Through our baptism, God promises to free us from our sins. When we go under the water, we believe that we died. We also believe that when we come out of the water, Christ lives in us:

> You are all sons of God through faith in Christ Jesus, **for all of you who <u>were baptized into Christ</u> have <u>clothed yourselves with Christ</u>**. There is neither Jew nor Greek, slave nor free, male nor female, **for you are all one in Christ Jesus.** (Ga.3:26-28 NIV)

Christ living in us is rebirth. The Spirit came down on Christ in His baptism. When we are baptized, the presence of Christ comes in us. We are changed, just like putting on a new set of clothes:

> My old self has been crucified with Christ. **It is no longer I who live, but <u>Christ lives in me</u>**. So I live in this earthly body <u>by trusting</u> in **the Son of God**, who loved me and gave himself for me. (Ga.2:20 NLT)

We might not always feel Christ living in us, but we must believe that He is. We must also believe that He will continue to change our attitudes, behavior, and character:

> **For you died**, and your life is now hidden with Christ in God. **When Christ, who is your life**, appears, then you also will appear with him in glory. (Co.3:3-4 NIV)

The heart of the Gospel is Christ living in us. Our change in character and behavior is the sign of being born again:

> **No-one who is born of God will continue to sin**, because God's seed remains in him; he **cannot go on sinning**, because he has been born of God. This is how we know who the children of God are and who the children of the devil are: **Anyone who does not do what is right is not a child of God**. (1Jn.3:9-10 NIV)

To stop doing wrong to others is good. However, to only focus on the actions and not destroy the cause behind our sin is useless. Sin will only resurface in another area of our lives. We need to deal with the cause of our sin by being born again. Our rebirth gives us the power to do what is right:

> If you know that He is righteous, **you know that everyone also who practices righteousness is born of Him**. (1Jn.2:29 NASB)

We are not born again by reaching a level of goodness. We are born again when Christ has control of our lives:

> My little children, for whom I am again **in the pain of childbirth until Christ is formed in you**, I wish I were present with you now and could change my tone, for **I am perplexed about you**. (Ga.4:19-20 NRSV)

Our spirit died when our first forefather ate the forbidden fruit. Our spirits are reborn when the Holy Spirit comes into our lives:

> **It is the Spirit who gives life; the flesh profits nothing**. The words that I speak to you are spirit, and they are life. (Jn.6:63 NKJV)

Therefore, before we can start sharing our message of truth, we need to be born again; otherwise, our sins will undo our message.

OUR MESSAGE

Many people have different ideas about Christianity. Since Christianity is a divine relationship between man and God, God's opinion is the only one that counts:

> *To them God willed to make known what are the riches of the glory of this mystery among the Gentiles: which is **Christ in you, the hope of glory**.*
> (Co.1:27 NKJV)

The only hope of heaven is Christ living in us. This is the message of the cross, and this is Christianity at the most basic level:

> *And the testimony is this, that God has given us eternal life, and this life is in His Son. **He who has the Son has the life**; he who does not have the Son of God **does not have the life**.* (1Jn.5:11-12 NASB)

God living in believers and the believers living in God is not something that comes with time. All believers have God living in them the moment they are born again of the Spirit:

> ***Whoever confesses*** *that Jesus is the Son of God,* ***God abides in him, and he in God.***
> (1Jn.4:15 NKJV)

The Corinthians could not understand that God lives in them and that they live in God. Twice Paul reminded the Corinthians that they were the temple of the Holy Spirit because God lived in them:

> ***Don't you know*** *that you yourselves are **God's temple** and that **God's Spirit lives in you**? If anyone destroys God's temple, God will destroy him; **for God's temple is sacred**, and you are that temple.*
> (1Co.3:16-17 NIV; 1Co.6:19-20)

Just like the Corinthians, many Christians today do not know that they are the temple of God. Salvation does not exist apart from being in God. This was God's plan from the beginning of time:

> *For **he chose us in him** before the creation of the world to be holy and blameless in his sight.* (Eph.1:4 NIV)

Christians were chosen to be in Him, and once in Him, we are saved. Christianity is set apart from all the other religions of the world because our God is not some "being" that we worship in some "place" far away. Our God personally lives in us, controlling our lives:

> ***In him* we were also chosen**, *having been predestined according to the plan of him who works out everything in conformity **with the purpose of his will.*** (Eph.1:11 NIV)

Even the forgiveness of sins rests upon being **in Christ:**

> ***In Him* we have redemption through His blood, the forgiveness of sins**, *according to the riches of His grace…* (Eph.1:7 NRSV)

Many churchgoers only believe that Christ died for their sins; but the Bible teaches that **in Him**, we take on His righteous character:

> *God made him who had no sin to be sin for us, so that **in him* we might become the righteousness of God**. (2Co.5:21 NIV)

Christianity was never meant to be a type of knowledge or a regular practice of religious ritual. Christianity is about us getting right with God so that we can have a relationship with God:

> *What agreement has **the temple of God** with idols? For **we are the temple** of the living God; as God said, "**I will live in them** and walk among them, and I will be their God, and they shall be my people."* (2Co.6:16 NRSV)

Through Jesus, we have regained a personal relationship with God:

> *Jesus replied, "All who love me will do what I say. My Father will love them, and **we will come and make our home with each of them**.* (Jn.14:23 NLT)

Through relationship, God teaches us His truths:

> *As for you, the anointing you received from him **remains in you**, and you do not need anyone to teach you. But as **his anointing teaches you about all things and as that anointing is real**, not counterfeit—just as it has taught you, **remain in him**.* (1Jn.2:27 NIV)

Do not be deceived; all Christians are in Christ:

> *And we know that the Son of God has come, and has given us understanding so that we may know Him who is true; and **we are in Him** who is true, **in His Son** Jesus Christ. This is **the true God** and eternal life.* (1Jn.5:20 NASB)

Christianity is centered on giving Christ control of our lives:

> *For '**In him** we live and **move** and **have our being'**; as even some of your own poets have said, 'For we too are his offspring.'* (Ac.17:28 NRSV)

The disciples could have tried to start their ministry without the Holy Spirit. However, people can only be used by God when they are controlled by Christ through the Holy Spirit:

> **Abide <u>in Me</u>, and I in you.** As the branch cannot bear fruit of itself unless **it abides in the vine**, so neither can you **unless you abide <u>in Me</u>**. I am the vine, you are the branches; **he who abides <u>in Me</u> and I in him**, he bears much fruit, **for <u>apart from Me</u> you can do nothing**.
> (Jn.15:4-5 NASB)

Christ died to be our Savior, but He arose to be our Lord by living in us. By Him living in us, we receive His power, love, wisdom, and holiness:

> For **<u>in him</u> the whole fullness of deity** dwells bodily, and you **have come to fullness <u>in him</u>**, who is the head of every ruler and authority.
> (Co.2:9-10 NRSV)

In Christ, and only in Him, can we have the fullness of God:

> For **<u>in him</u>** you have been enriched in **<u>every</u>** way— in all your speaking and in **<u>all</u>** your knowledge— because our testimony about Christ was confirmed in you. Therefore **you do not lack <u>any</u> spiritual gift** as you eagerly wait for our Lord Jesus Christ to be revealed. (1Co.1:5-7 NIV)

Since Christ lives in us with all His fullness, what does a Christian lack? All God's promises are "yes" for all who are in Christ:

> For the Son of God, Jesus Christ, who was preached among you by me and Silas and Timothy, was not "Yes" and "No," but **<u>in him</u> it has always been "Yes."** For **no matter how many promises God has made, they are "Yes" <u>in Christ</u>**. And so through him the "Amen" is spoken by us to the glory of God. Now **it is God who makes both us and you stand firm in Christ**.
> (2Co.1:19-20 NIV)

Many Christians live spiritually poor lives because they live out a religion instead of living in Christ. All the blessings of God are in Christ:

> And my **God will supply all your needs** according to His riches in glory **<u>in Christ</u> Jesus**.
> (Php.4:19 NIV)

If Christ lives in us with the fullness of God, then we will succeed in serving Him:

> And God is able to make **all grace** abound to you, so that in **all things** at **all times**, having **all that you need**, you will **abound in every good work**.
> (2Co.9:8 NIV)

There is no reason why a Christian should fail in living to please God because Christ cannot fail! Since Christ lives in us and controls our lives, our lives should reflect the person of Christ:

> *My little children, for whom I am again in the pain of childbirth **until Christ is formed in you**...* (Ga.4:19 NASB)

Paul was waiting for the Galatians to be changed and become like Christ. Being changed to act like Christ is the proof that we are a Christian:

> ***God is love**, and all who **live in love live in God, and God lives in them**. And as we live in God, our love grows more perfect. So we will not be afraid on the day of judgment, but we can face him with confidence because **we live like Jesus here in this world**.* (1Jn.4:16-17 NIV)

Jesus lived a perfect life—a life without sin. If Jesus lives in us, we will sin less and less each day. He will reveal Himself in us:

> *But you know that he appeared so that he might take away our sins. And **in him** is no sin. No one **who lives in him** keeps on sinning. No one who continues to sin has either seen him or **known him**.* (1Jn.3:5-6 NIV)

Since Christ lives in Christians, we will keep changing to become more like Him. We will never be perfect; but we will always be under construction—becoming more holy each day. Our sinful nature is gone the moment we are in Christ:

> ***Those who belong to Christ** Jesus **have** crucified the sinful nature with its passions and desires.* (Ga.5:24 NIV)

We must ask God to continue to take away the traces of sin in our lives that are left over from our former way of life:

> *Therefore, brothers, we have an obligation— but it is not to the sinful nature, to live according to it. For **if you live according to the sinful nature**, you will die; but **if by the Spirit you put to death the misdeeds of the body**, you will live, because **those who are led by the Spirit of God** are sons of God.* (Ro.8:12-14 NIV)

Christ's Spirit puts to death the sins of our past. We do many things because of habit—a repeated behavior for a long time. Some of these habits are not evil but merely ways to approach tasks. For example, I have been married to my wife for over thirty years. I know what pleases her and what makes her angry. I strive to live in harmony with my wife. If she died and I remarried, out of habit I would try to please my second wife like I pleased my first wife. However, the habits that pleased my first wife could very well displease my second wife because the two women are different. Because I would not want to anger my second wife, I would need to learn new habits that would please her—a process that takes time. Similarly, before we were saved, we lived to please the sinful nature for a long time. Its sinful actions became habits. Even though we are born again in an instant, we need time to learn both what displeases God and new ways to please Him. For this reason, we will never be perfect, but we will always be changing as we grow in our relationship with God. Since Christ lives in us, we will become more like Him. Christ did exactly what His Father commanded Him. We too will do what the Father wants, just like Christ did:

> Now he who **keeps His commandments** abides **in Him**, **and He in him**. And by this we know that He abides in us, **by the Spirit** whom He has given us. (1Jn.3:24 NKJV)

Therefore, we are saved by Christ living in us through the presence of the Holy Spirit. God controls and changes our lives to be like Him in our attitudes, behavior, and character—a process which will continue the rest of our lives.

OUR MOTIVE

Sometimes the news will report a medical breakthrough. The breakthrough offers hope for many people who are suffering from a certain disease. When these people hear about the new cure, they pass it on to others to give hope to those who share in their suffering. In the same way, we who are spiritually sick should want to share the cure for habitual sin. Step 12 is just passing the message: "This worked for me!"

> Jesus said to the people who believed in him, "You are truly my disciples **if you remain faithful to my teachings**. And you will know the truth, and **the truth will set you free**." (Jn.8:31-32 NLT)

Christ's teachings are not only true, but they also contain the power to free us from our slavery to sin:

> For I am not ashamed of the gospel, **for it is the power of God for salvation to everyone who believes**, to the Jew first and also to the Greek. (Ro.1:16 NASB)

Paul experienced the life-changing power of God, and he had to tell others about it. Being freed from habitual sin moves us to reach out to others who also suffer from habitual sin. Knowing the lack of hope from our past creates in us not only compassion but also the desire to share the good news:

> However, I consider my life worth nothing to me, if only I may finish the race and complete the task the Lord Jesus has given me--**the task of testifying to the gospel of God's grace**. .... Therefore, I declare to you today that **I am innocent of the blood of all men**. For **I have not hesitated to proclaim to you the whole will of God**. (Ac.20:24&27 NIV)

Paul did not carry the guilt of other men's souls because he told the good news to everyone who would listen. We are also called to be a light in this dark world:

> **You are the light of the world.** A city that is set on a hill cannot be hidden. Nor do they light a lamp and put it under a basket, but on a lampstand, and **it gives light to all who are in the house**.
> (Mt.5:14-15 NKJV)

As light, we point to the cross as the only cure to life's problem of sin:

> Conduct yourselves with wisdom toward outsiders, **making the most of the opportunity**. Let your speech always be with grace, as though seasoned with salt, **so that you will know how you should respond to each person.** (Co.4:5-6 NASB)

We must always be willing, prepared, and ready to share this message of hope:

> But in your hearts set apart Christ as Lord. **Always be prepared to give an answer to everyone who asks you to give the reason for the hope that you have**. But do this with gentleness and respect, keeping a clear conscience. (1Pe.3:15-16 NIV)

If someone silently overcomes habitual sin but never tells others that it was done by Christ, other people will never know how they can gain victory. Through our obedience to share the message, we will receive a greater blessing:

> I pray **that you may be active in sharing your faith**, so that **you will <u>have a full understanding</u> of every good thing we have in Christ**.
> (Phm.1:6 NIV)

Through our sharing, we better understand all that Christ has done for us. Through sharing, we are also giving Christ the credit for what He has done:

> **If you confess with your mouth the Lord Jesus** and believe in your heart that God has raised Him from the dead, **you will be saved**. For with the

> heart one believes unto righteousness, and **with the mouth confession is made unto salvation.** (Ro.10:9-10 NKJV)

We need to share the Gospel; but we need to know when and to whom we must share it:

> Since **we are living by the Spirit**, let us **follow the Spirit's leading in every part of our lives.** (Ga.5:25 NLT)

When some people gain victory over sin, they share their experience with everyone they meet. However, not everyone is ready to hear about what Christ did for us. This application could cause us to offend many. To some, sharing the Gospel is like picking apples. Just like people pick all the apples on a tree at one time, some people may want to tell everyone they meet about the change in their life. However, sharing the good news of Christ is more like picking peaches. When I worked in an orchard, I did not pick every peach on a tree but looked at the color to tell which peaches were ripe. I would come back to the same tree many times, picking only the fruit that was ready. In the same way, we need to listen to the Spirit's leading regarding whom we should share our story with. The Spirit will let us know who is ripe for the Gospel. It is not the force of our words or the smoothness of our speech that moves people's hearts; it is God's Spirit:

> A certain woman named Lydia, a worshiper of God, was listening to us; she was from the city of Thyatira and a dealer in purple cloth. **The Lord opened her heart to listen eagerly to what was said by Paul.** (Ac.16:14 NRSV)

Just as our hearts were evil and turned away from God, other people's hearts are evil too. For this reason, we must work within God's timing; for He is the One Who makes the heart ready for His message:

> **All that the Father gives me will come to me**, and whoever comes to me I will never drive away... **"No one can come to me unless the Father who sent me draws him,** and I will raise him up at the last day... He went on to say, "This is why I told you that **no one can come to me unless the Father has enabled him."** (Jn. 6:37, 44-65 NIV)

Without God working in people's hearts, no one will turn to Him. Christians are a result of God's work—there are no self-made Christians:

> For we are **what he has made us**, **created in Christ** Jesus for good works, which God prepared beforehand to be our way of life.

(Eph.2:10 NRSV)

We do not become Christian because we are so smart or clever; we become Christians by God working in our lives:

> Dear friends, you always followed my instructions when I was with you. And now that I am away, it is even more important. Work hard to show the results of your salvation, obeying God with deep reverence and fear. **For God is working in you, <u>giving you the desire and the power</u> to do what pleases him.** (Php.2:12-13 NLT)

Only by God's grace are we able to make right choices. He is the One Who chose us, worked in us, and enabled us to turn to Him:

> **You did not choose Me but I chose you, and appointed you** that you would go and bear fruit, and that your fruit would remain. (Jn.15:16 NASB)

Since it is Christ Who chose us, it is Christ Who must choose others. Our sharing the Gospel must be done with Christ's leading:

> And **<u>the Lord added</u> to the church daily those who were being saved**. (Ac.2:47 NKJV)

What we think of people can be misleading, because accepting the Gospel is not a matter of people's abilities. Many times those whom the world would think the least likely to turn to Christ accept Him:

> **He chose the lowly things of this world** and the despised things—and the things that are not—to nullify the things that are, so that no-one may boast before him. **It is because of him that you are in Christ Jesus**, who has become for us wisdom from God—that is, our righteousness, holiness and redemption. Therefore, as it is written: "**Let him who boasts boast in the Lord.**" (1Co.1:28-31 NIV)

We must listen to God regarding whom we should share the Gospel with. Otherwise, our sharing will not lead anyone to Christ and a changed life:

> Now when the Gentiles heard this, they were glad and glorified the word of the Lord. And **as many as had been appointed to eternal life believed**. (Ac.13:48 NKJV)

Therefore, we must tell others that it is only by being **in Christ** that we **have been freed** from the sins that had enslaved us.

For Further Thought:

Being born again is when...

1. Why must we be spiritually born again before we can share the good news with others?

2. What must happen before we can be born again?

3. What difference does being born again make in your life?

4. What sums up the Christian life?

5. Why should we share the good news?

6. Why must we listen to God to know with whom we should share?

7. What part does God play in a person's freedom from sin?

Memory Verse:
> *Be wise in the way you act toward outsiders; make the most of every opportunity.*   Colossians.4:5

NOTES:

Appendix

Romans 7

My Life

    Early in my Christian life, my spiritual growth was greatly hindered in overcoming sin because many taught that Romans 7:7-25 describes the normal Christian life. When I was a young Christian, I tried to overcome my sins by sheer determination. I struggled to overcome a habitual sin and to maintain that victory. Satan used a fellow Christian to point out that even Paul could not achieve victory over sin in Romans 7:7-25. Discouraged, I lost my zeal for perfection and fell into sin once again. I was continually frustrated and defeated during the first years of my Christian life. These years of defeat could have been prevented if someone had taught me the true context of Romans 7:7-25. In this appendix, we will consider to whom Paul addressed Romans 7:7-25 and discover its true meaning in order to find freedom from habitual sin. Jesus said:

> *Jesus said to the people who believed in him, "You are truly my disciples **if you remain faithful to my teachings**. And you **will know the truth, and the truth will set you free**."*   (Jn.8:31-32 NLT)

Therefore, let us consider the truth about Romans 7.

The Address

    The letter to the Roman church was one long letter without the chapters or verses that now divide it. Chapters and verses were added much later for the benefit of study. When I read Romans 7:1, I noticed that Paul singled out one group within the church at Rome:

> *"Do you not know, brothers—**for I am speaking to <u>men who know the Law</u>**- that **the law has** authority over a man only as long as he lives."*
>   (Ro.7:1 NIV)

The Roman church contained Jewish and Gentile believers (Ac.18:2). However, Paul could not be addressing Romans 7:7-25 to the Gentile believers because they do not know God's Law:

> For when **Gentiles who do not have the Law** do instinctively the things of the Law, **these, not having the Law**, are a law to themselves.
> (Ro.2:14 NASB; Ps 147:20)

Gentiles do not have the Law. Nor could Paul have been addressing Christians in Romans 7:7-25, because they are not under Law but under grace:

> Shall we sin because **we are not under law but under grace**? Certainly not!
> (Ro.6:15 NKJV)

Once we became Christians, we were no longer under the Law:

> **For Christ is the end of the law** so that there may be righteousness for everyone who believes.
> (Ro.10:4 NRSV; Ga.5:18)

The purpose of the Law is to convince people that they are sinners and that they need a Savior. When we became Christians, we died to the Law:

> So, my brothers, **you also died to the law** through the body of Christ, that you might belong to another, to him who was raised from the dead, in order that we might bear fruit to God. . . . But now, **by dying to what once bound us, we have been released from the law** so that we serve in the new way of the Spirit, and **not in the old way of the written code**.
> (Ro.7:4&6 NIV; Ro.6:14-15)

The only people group that Paul could be addressing is the Jews who converted to Christianity. Before a Jew became a Christian, he tried to obey the Law in order to be accepted by God. In Romans 7:7-25, Paul described what the Jews experienced living under the Law:

> But if you bear **the name "Jew"** and **rely upon the Law** and boast in God, and know His will and approve the things that are essential, **being instructed out of the Law**.
> (Ro.2:17-18 NASB; Ro.2:17-29; Ro.3:9-20)

Since only the Jews knew the Law, Paul definitely addressed Romans 7 to the Jewish Christians. Paul wanted to remind the Jewish Christians that living by Law was not only powerless but also different than living by the Holy Spirit. Because the Jews lived by the Law, only a person who was formerly a Jew could answer the question that sets the tone for the rest of Romans 7:

> *What shall we say then?* ***Is the law sin?*** (Ro.7:7 NKJV)

Since the man of Romans 7:7-25 lives by the Law, he does not have God's grace. All Christians live by grace, which is contrary to the Law. Hence, the man described in Romans 7:7-25 is not a Christian because he lives under Law instead of grace:

> ***You are not under law*** *but* ***under grace.*** (Ro.6:14 NASB)

If a person claims to be a Christian but lives by the Law, he is not only void of grace but also void of Christ Himself:

> *You who are trying to be* ***justified*** ***by law*** *have been* ***alienated from Christ****; you have* ***fallen away from grace****. But* ***by faith*** *we eagerly* ***await through the Spirit the righteousness*** *for which we hope.* (Ga.5:4-5 NIV)

Living by Law prevents churchgoers from experiencing the presence of Christ. The Holy Spirit indwells Christians and enables them to overcome sin. Since the person of Romans 7:7-25 cannot overcome his sin, he does not have the Holy Spirit during this experience. Paul was describing his pre-conversion experience under the Law:

> *But* ***if*** *you are led by the Spirit,* ***you are not under the law****.* (Ga.5:18 NKJV)

Therefore, Paul addressed Romans 7 to Jews, "men who know the Law" (Ro.7:1), to prove the powerlessness of living by the Law. Because Christians do not live by the Law, they are excluded from the experience that Paul described in Romans 7:7-25.

THE CONTEXT

The context of Romans 7:7-25 provides one of the greatest arguments to prove that this Scripture does not describe Paul's Christian experience but rather his Jewish life under the Law. When we compare statements in Romans 7:7-25 to statements in Romans 6 and 8, we find that Paul directly contradicted himself. Either Paul did not know what he was writing about, or he was addressing two different time periods of his life. Consider the following comparisons.

First, the man described in Romans 7:7-25 is living under the Law:

- *For I would not have known covetousness* ***unless*** ***the law*** *had said,* "*You* shall not covet." (Ro.7:7 NKJV)

- I agree that **the law is good**. (Ro.7:16 NKJV)
- **For I delight in the law of God** according to the inward man.
  (Ro. 7:22 NKJV)
- So then, with the mind **I myself serve the law of God**. (Ro.7:25 NKJV)

The man in Romans 7:7-25 is obviously living by the Law. **In these 18 verses, the word "law" is used 15 times; and the word "commandment" is used 7 times**. Since the Law is the central theme, Paul could not be describing his Christian experience in Romans 7:7-25 as Christians are not under the Law. Paul told the Roman Christians in the previous chapter:

- For sin shall not be master over you, **for you are not under law** but under grace. (Ro.6:14 NASB)
- What then? Shall we sin because **we are not under law** but under grace? May it never be! (Ro.6:15 NASB)
- In the same way, my friends, **you have died to the law through the body of Christ**. (Ro.7:4 NRSV)
- But now **we have been released from the Law**, having died to that by which we were bound... (Ro.7:6 NASB)

Therefore, since the man described in Romans 7:7-25 is trying to please God by keeping the Law, he is not a Christian because Christians are no longer under the Law.

Second, the man described in Romans 7:7-25 was considered **dead** while living under the Law with its commands:

- **I was alive once** without the law, but when the commandment came, sin revived and **I died**. (Ro.7:9 NKJV)
- And the commandment, which was to bring life, **I found to bring death**. (Ro.7:10 NKJV)
- The commandment, deceived me, and through the commandment **put me to death**. (Ro.7:11 NIV)
- What wretched man that I am! Who will deliver me from **this body of death**? (Ro.7:24 NKJV)

The man in Romans 7:7-25 could not be a Christian because a Christian is considered alive; eternal life begins when we are born again:

- Just as Christ was raised from the dead by the glory of the Father, even so **we also should walk in <u>newness of life</u>**. (Ro.6:4 NKJV)
- Likewise you also, reckon yourselves to be dead indeed to sin, but **<u>alive</u> to God in Christ** Jesus our Lord. (Ro.6:11 NKJV)
- Present yourselves to God **as being <u>alive from the dead</u>**, and your members as instruments of righteousness to God. (Ro.6:13 NKJV)
- For the wages of sin is death, but **the gift of God <u>is eternal life</u>** in Christ Jesus our Lord. (Ro.6:23 NKJV)
- The mind of sinful man is death, but **the mind controlled by the Spirit <u>is life</u>** and peace. (Ro.8:6 NIV)
- He who raised Christ from the dead **<u>will also give life</u> to your mortal bodies** through His Spirit who dwells in you. (Ro.8:11 NKJV)

The man in Romans 7 is dead, but the man of Romans 6 and 8 is alive. Therefore, since the man described in Romans 7 is dead and not alive, he could not be a Christian.

Third, the man described in Romans 7:7-25 is still living under the power of sin:

- When the commandment came, **<u>sin became alive</u> and I died**. (Ro.7:9 NASB)
- So I am not the one doing wrong; **it is sin living in me that does it**. (Ro.7:17 NLT)
- It is no longer I who do it, but **it is <u>sin living in me</u>** that does it. (Ro.7:20 NIV)

The man of Romans 7:7-25 still has sin living in him, but Paul and the Roman Christians in Romans 6 and 8 are dead to the power of sin:

- How shall **we who died to sin** live any longer in it? (Ro.6:2 NKJV)
- Even so **consider yourselves to be dead to sin**, but alive to God in Christ Jesus. (Ro.6:11 NASB)
- God declared **an end to sin's control over us** by giving his Son as a sacrifice for our sins. (Ro.8:3 NLT)

The power of sin is still alive in the man in Romans 7; however, sin is declared dead in Christians in Romans 6 and 8. Therefore, since sin is alive in the man of Romans 7, he cannot be a Christian.

Fourth, the man in Romans 7:7-25 is controlled by the power of sin. The power of sin deceived him, seized him, and produced wicked behavior in him:

- *We know that the law is spiritual; but I am unspiritual, **sold as <u>a slave to sin</u>**.* (Ro.7:14 NIV)
- *But sin, **<u>seizing</u>** the opportunity afforded by the commandment, **<u>produced in me</u>** all kinds of covetousness.* (Ro.7:8 NRSV)
- *For sin, **<u>seizing</u>** the opportunity afforded by the commandment, **<u>deceived me</u>** and through it **<u>killed</u>** me.* (Ro.7:11 NRSV)
- *So I am not the one doing wrong; it is **sin living in me that <u>does it</u>**.* (Ro.7:17 NLT)
- *But if **I do what I don't want to do**, I am not really the one doing wrong; it is **sin living in me that <u>does it</u>**.* (Ro.7:20 NLT)

Before the Jewish Christians accepted Christ, they were still under the Law, allowing the power of sin to seize and control them:

> **The power of sin <u>is the law</u>.** (1Co.15:56 NASB)

However, Christians are no longer under the Law and thereby are freed through Christ from their slavery to the power of sin:

- *For **<u>sin shall not be master</u> over you**, for you are not under law but under grace.* (Ro 6:14 NASB)
- *Our old man was crucified with Him, that the body of sin might be done away with, **that we should <u>no longer be slaves of sin</u>**.* (Ro.6:6 NKJV)
- *For whoever **has died is <u>freed from sin</u>**.* (Ro.6:7 NRSV)
- *But thanks be to God **that though you <u>were slaves of sin</u>**...* (Ro.6:17 NASB)
- *You, having been **<u>set free from sin</u>**, have become slaves of righteousness.* (Ro.6:18 NRSV)
- *For **when you <u>were slaves of sin</u>**, . . .* (Ro.6:20 NASB)
- *But now that you have been **<u>set free from sin</u>** and have become slaves to God . . .* (Ro.6:22 NRSV)

Christ purchased Christians from their old master, sin, so that they could become slaves to righteousness—slaves to God:

- *Having been freed from sin, you **became slaves of righteousness**.* (Ro.6:18 NASB)

- But now having been set free from sin, and **having become** slaves of God
  ... (Ro.6:22 NKJV)

A person can be owned by only one master at a time. Sin is the master of the man in Romans 7, but Christians are declared freed from sin and have become slaves of God in Romans 6. Therefore, since the man of Romans 7 is controlled by sin, he cannot be a Christian.

Fifth, the man of Romans 7:7-25 denies that the Holy Spirit lives in him:

- We know that the law is spiritual; but **I am unspiritual**. (Ro.7:14 NIV)
- For I know that **nothing good dwells in me**. (Ro.7:18 NASB)

The Holy Spirit is good. Since nothing good lives in the man of Romans 7:7-25, this man is obviously void of the Holy Spirit. Also, Paul never mentioned the Holy Spirit in Romans 7:7-25 but stated that he was unspiritual. In this passage, the man described has not given Christ control of his life. This man is still in control of his own life. He used the pronouns "I" 32 times and "me" 11 times, indicating that he tried to attain holiness by his own strength. Therefore, the man of Romans 7:7-25 has not experienced the Holy Spirit. The Holy Spirit is not mentioned in this passage. However, when Paul addressed the Christians in Romans 8, he taught them that the Holy Spirit lived in them. Romans 8 mentioned the Holy Spirit 18 times:

- The righteous requirement of the law might be fulfilled in us who do not walk according to the flesh but **according to the Spirit**. (Ro.8:4 NKJV)
- ... **those who live according to the Spirit** set their minds on the things of the Spirit. (Ro.8:5 NASB)
- **The mind set on the Spirit** is life and peace. (Ro.8:6 NASB)
- Now **if anyone does not have the Spirit of Christ, he is not His**. (Ro.8:9 NKJV)
- He who raised Christ from the dead will also give life to your mortal bodies **through His Spirit who dwells in you**. (Ro.8:11 NASB)
- If **by the Spirit** you put to death the deeds of the body, you will live. (Ro.8:13 NKJV)

The Holy Spirit does not live in the man of Romans 7; however, Paul taught that the Holy Spirit lives in Christians in Romans 8. Therefore, since the man of Romans 7 does not have the Holy Spirit living in him, he cannot be a Christian.

Sixth, the man described in Romans 7:7-25 is still under the control of the sinful nature (flesh):

- And I know that nothing good lives in me, that is, **in my sinful nature**. (Ro.7:18 NLT)
- So then, I myself in my mind am a slave to God's law, **but in the sinful nature** a slave to the law of sin. (Ro.7:25 NIV)

Everyone is controlled by the sinful nature until he is born again by the Holy Spirit. A person cannot be controlled by the sinful nature one moment and then controlled by the Holy Spirit the next moment. A person is either one of **those** controlled by the sinful nature or one of **those** controlled by the Holy Spirit:

- <u>**Those**</u> **who live according to the sinful nature** have their minds set on what that nature desires; **but** <u>**those**</u> **who live in accordance with the Spirit** have their minds set on what the Spirit desires. (Ro.8:5 NIV)
- That's why those **who are still under the control of their sinful nature** can never please God. **But you are <u>not controlled</u> by your sinful nature. You <u>are controlled</u> by the Spirit** if you have the Spirit of God living in you. (And remember that those who do not have the Spirit of Christ living in them do not belong to him at all.) (Ro.8:8-9 NLT)
- For **if you live** according **to the sinful nature, <u>you will die</u>**; but **if by the Spirit** you put to death the misdeeds of the body, <u>**you will live**</u>. (Ro.8:13 NIV)

Christians do not live according to the sinful nature, for the Holy Spirit displaced it:

- For when we <u>**were controlled**</u> by the sinful nature... (Ro.7:5 NIV)
- ...who **<u>do not live according</u> to the sinful nature** but according to the Spirit. (Ro.8:4 NIV)
- Therefore, brothers, we have an obligation—but **it is <u>not to the sinful nature</u>**, to live according to it. (Ro.8:12 NIV)

The Bible is clear. For the Christian, his sinful nature has been crucified:

- Those who belong to Christ Jesus **<u>have crucified</u> the sinful nature** with its passions and desires. (Ga.5:24 NIV)

- **When you came to Christ, you were "circumcised,"** but not by a physical procedure. Christ performed a spiritual circumcision—**the cutting away of your sinful nature**. (Co.2:11 NLT)

The sinful nature is still alive in the man of Romans 7, but it is declared dead for Christians in Romans 8. Therefore, since the man of Romans 7 is not dead to the sinful nature, he cannot be a Christian.

Seventh, the man described in Romans 7:7-25 is still under the law of sin:

- ...making me **a prisoner of the law of sin** which is in my members. (Ro.7:23 NASB)
- So then, **I myself** in my mind **am** a slave to God's law, but in the sinful nature **a slave to the law of sin**. (Ro.7:25 NIV)

Christ freed Christians from the law of sin and placed them under the law of the Holy Spirit:

- For the **law of the Spirit** of life in Christ **Jesus has set you free from the law of sin** and of death. (Ro.8:2 NASB)

The man in Romans 7 is still under the law of sin and death, but Paul taught that Christians are not under the law of sin and death in Roman's 8. Therefore, since the man of Romans 7 still lives under the law of sin, he cannot be a Christian.

If we interpret Romans 7:7-25 to be the normal Christian life, then we have some serious problems with context. These problems are resolved if in Romans 7:7-25 Paul was describing his former life under the Law. This Scripture was meant to show a Jew the powerlessness of continuing to live by the Law. Therefore, the contradictions between Romans 7:7-25 and Romans 6 and 8 support the interpretation that Paul used these chapters to describe two different periods in his life: pre-conversion under the Law and post-conversion under the Holy Spirit.

THE USE OF PRONOUNS

Paul's choice of pronouns gives further support that Romans 7:7-25 does not describe the Christian experience. Paul used different pronouns in Romans 7:7-25 than he used in Romans 6:1-7:6 and Romans 8. When we examine Paul's use of pronouns, we clearly see that

Paul described the Christian experience (Ro.6:1-7:6), then spoke of his former Jewish experience under the Law (Ro.7:7-25), and then finally continued to describe the Christian experience (Ro.8). In Romans 6:1-7:6 and Romans 8, Paul used plural pronouns to show that the church at Rome shared his Christian experience. However, in Romans 7:7-25, Paul stopped using plural pronouns and only used singular pronouns to answer the question, "Is the Law sin?" Prior to Romans 7:7, we read:

> For **when we were** controlled by the sinful nature, the sinful passions aroused by the Law were at work in **our** bodies, so that **we** bore fruit for death. But now, by dying to what once bound **us**, **we** have been released from the Law so that **we** serve in the new way of the Spirit, and not in the old way of the written code. (Ro.7:5-6 NIV)

We know that both Paul and the Roman church experienced the previous verses because Paul used the inclusive pronoun "we." In Romans 7:7-25, Paul used singular pronouns (I, me) to indicate that he was writing his personal experience, not an experience that the Roman Christians shared with him:

> "*I* do not understand what *I* do. For what *I* want to do *I* do not do, but what *I* hate *I* do." (Ro.7:15 NIV)

Paul could have included the Roman Christians in his experience by writing:

> **We** do not understand what **we** do. For what **we** want to do **we** do not do, but what **we** hate **we** do. **(Not Scripture)**

But Paul did not use "we." Again, let me point out that Paul used the word "I" 32 times and the word "me" 11 times in Romans 7:7-25, indicating that the Roman church did not share this experience. Consequently, Paul used the singular pronoun in Romans 7:7-25 to illustrate his personal experience in Jewish life. He taught that the Law was not sin but that he was controlled by sin. We know that Paul chose pronouns meaningfully because in Romans 7:14 he used the only plural pronoun in this chapter and then switched back to the singular pronoun "I":

> For **we know** that the law is spiritual; but **I am** of the flesh, sold into the bondage of sin. (Ro.7:14 NASB)

In the previous verse, Paul used a plural pronoun to acknowledge a Christian truth that he shared with the Roman Christians and then resumed using a singular pronoun to finish his description of his Jewish experience. Therefore, the change in pronouns gives support that Paul wrote Romans 7:7-25 to describe his former personal life as a Jew under the Law.

THE TENSES

Some people believe that Romans 7:7-25 must refer to Paul's Christian experience because Paul used verbs that are in the present tense. However, in Romans 7:7-25, Paul used the present tense that is called the "historical presents." The Greek language uses the historical presents tense so that readers will think that they are experiencing a past event as it unfolded. Likewise, Paul used the historical presents tense so that the Jew and Gentile Christians could understand the frustration that he experienced under the Law. Even though the sincere Jews loved God's Law, they were slaves to sin. Hence, they disobeyed the Law. The Paul of Romans 7:7-25 **always** did bad and could not do good:

> For we know that the Law is spiritual, but **I am** of flesh, sold into bondage to sin. For what **I am** doing, **I do** not understand; for **I am** not practicing what **I would like to** do, but **I am** doing the very thing I hate.
> (Ro.7:14-15 NASB)

When Paul wrote Romans 7:7-25, he was a Christian and not under the Law. Hence, Romans 7:7-25 described Paul's former experience as a Jew under the Law. Paul used the historical presents tense so that his readers could understand his personal experience that he lived in the past. The historical presents tense was also used in Ephesians:

> You **were taught**, with regard to **your former way of life**, to **put off your old self**, which **is being corrupted** by its deceitful desires; **to be** made new in the attitude of your minds; and **to put on** the new self, created **to be** like God **in true righteousness and holiness**. (Eph.4:22-24 NIV)

Even though Paul began the previous verses in the past tense, he switched to the present tense: "is being corrupted." In Ephesians 4:22-24, Paul used the historical presents tense to contrast the holiness of a Christian's life with the corruption of man's sinful nature. According to Romans 6, we know that our old self (sinful nature) is dead because we died with Christ:

> *We know that our <u>old self</u> was crucified with him* so that the body of sin might be destroyed, and we might no longer be enslaved to sin. For whoever has died is freed from sin. (Ro.6:6-7 NRSV)

Therefore, in Romans 7:7-25, Paul described his former way of life but used the historical presents tense to show the frustration he had experienced while living under the Law.

THE CONCEPTS

Finally, if Romans 7:7-25 does not describe a Jew's life under the Law, then it teaches that Christians will always do bad and will not be able to do good. However, throughout the Scriptures, God urges us to live holy lives that imitate Christ's life. For instance, Paul mentioned the holiness that Christ worked in his life and in the lives of his fellow workers:

> You are witnesses, and so is God, of **how holy, righteous and blameless we were among you** who believed. (1Th.2:10 NIV)

Paul reminded the Corinthians of how he lived his Christian life:

> Our conscience testifies that we have conducted ourselves in the world, and especially in our relations with you, **in the holiness and sincerity that are from God**. (2Co.1:12 NIV)

The previous two Scriptures are incongruent with Romans 7:7-25 which describes total defeat and hopeless submission to sin:

> And I know that nothing good lives in me, that is, in my sinful nature. **I want to** do what is right, **<u>but I can't</u>**. **I want to** do what is good, **<u>but I don't</u>**. **I don't want** to do what is wrong, but **<u>I do it anyway</u>**. (Ro.7:18-19 NLT)

If Paul was describing his Christian life, there is no hope for the alcoholic, the drug addict, the sexually immoral, or the common sinner. When Paul addressed the churches in his letters, did he call them sinners?

> Paul, an apostle of Christ Jesus by the will of God, To **the sinners** in Ephesus, **the unfaithful** in Christ Jesus. **(Not Scripture)**

Paul **never** referred to Christians by the Greek word "hamartolos"— "sinners." Instead, we read:

> Paul, an apostle of Christ Jesus by the will of God, **To <u>the saints</u>** who are at Ephesus and **who are faithful** in Christ Jesus. (Eph.1:1 NASB)

Paul always referred to Christians by the Greek word "hagios"—"saints." "Hagios" is also used to describe the Spirit of God: the "Hagios" Spirit (Holy Spirit). Notice the verb tense in the following verse:

> But God demonstrates His own love toward us, in that **while we were yet sinners**, Christ died for us. (Ro.5:8 NASB)

We were sinners bound for hell **before** we came to Christ:

> He who **turns a sinner from the error** of his way **will save** his soul from death and will cover a multitude of sins. (Ja.5:20 NASB)

Sinners are not already saved. Paul was the worst of sinners, but he was shown mercy when he was saved through Christ:

> Here is a trustworthy saying that deserves full acceptance: Christ **Jesus came into the world to save sinners--of whom I am the worst**. But for that very reason **I was shown** mercy so that in me, the worst of sinners, Christ Jesus might display his unlimited patience **as an example for those who would believe on him** and receive eternal life.
> (1Ti.1:15-16 NIV)

Christians are no longer sinners enslaved to sin. They are saints who sometimes fall into sin.

> My dear children, **I write this to you so that you will not sin**. But **if anybody does sin**, we have one who speaks to the Father in our defence—Jesus Christ, the Righteous One. (1Jn.2:1 NIV)

The man of Romans 7:7-25 cries out to God because of his helplessness and hopelessness:

> What a wretched man I am! **Who will rescue** me from this body of death? (Ro.7:24 NIV)

Notice the future tense: "Who will rescue me." Hence, the Paul of Romans 7:7-25 has not yet been rescued, but he wants to be rescued. In the next verse, Paul states the solution to his wickedness:

> Thanks be to God **through Jesus Christ our Lord!** (Ro.7:25 NASB)

Christ came to rescue the Jews from their hopeless situation. In Romans 7:7-25, Paul summarized the Jews' experience under the Law:

> So then, **I myself** in my mind am a slave to God's law, but **in the sinful nature a slave to the law of sin**. (Ro.7:25 NIV)

We know that Romans 7:7-25 describes a Jew's experience under the Law because of the previous arguments. The "therefore" at the beginning of Romans 8:1 reflects back to Romans 7:25:

> *Thanks be to God **through Jesus Christ our Lord**!* (Ro.7:25 NASB)

> ***There is therefore now** no condemnation to those **who are in Christ Jesus**, who do not walk according to the flesh, but according to the Spirit. For the law of the Spirit **of life in Christ Jesus** has **made me free from the law of sin and death**.* (Ro.8:1-2 NKJV)

There is no reason to continue in the experience of Romans 7:7-25. Take God's Word to heart today. Through Jesus Christ, we have received grace, which strengthens us, and the Holy Spirit, Who transforms us and enables us to overcome the experience of Romans 7:

> *So, my brothers, you also <u>died to the law</u> through the body of Christ, that you might belong to another, to him who was raised from the dead, in order that we might bear fruit to God. For **when we <u>were controlled</u>** by the sinful nature, **the sinful passions <u>aroused by the law</u> were at work in our bodies**, so that we bore fruit for death. But now, by dying to what once bound us, **we h<u>ave been released from the law</u> so that we serve in <u>the new way</u> of the Spirit**, and not in the old way of the written code.* (Ro.7:4-6 NIV)

FOR FURTHER THOUGHT:

Romans 7 is addressed to...

1. How was a person's relationship to the Law changed after becoming a Christian?

2. Are Christians dead or alive in Christ?

3. Are Christians a slave to the power of sin, and if not, whom do they serve?

4. Can a person be a Christian and not have the Holy Spirit living in him?

5. Give Scriptures that support whether the sinful nature is or is not alive in a Christian?

6. Why did Paul only use personal pronouns to describe his experience in Romans 7:7:25?

7. How can Paul use the present tense to describe a past experience in Ephesians 4:22?

8. What were Paul and his missionary team known for when they lived among the people?

Memory Verse:
What a wretched man I am! Who will rescue me from this body of death? Thanks be to God—through Jesus Christ our Lord! Romans 7:24-24 NIV

NOTES:

About the Author

Ron joined the military at the age of seventeen with the hope of adventure. On the flight to boot camp, he heard God's voice: "Ron, are you going to live the rest of your life for yourself, or are you going to live for Me?" By the time the plane landed, Ron made Christ both his Savior and Lord. During his time in the service, he was nicknamed "reverend" because of the radical change in his attitude, behavior, and character. After an honorable discharge, Ron has endeavored to serve his Lord Jesus Christ in instant, absolute obedience. Christians first recognized Ron's prophetic gift while he was working in the inner city. His heart was broken by the church's apathy to the poor and by Christianity's conformity to the world. The Bible defines the gift of prophecy:

> And if I have **the gift of prophecy**, and know **all mysteries and all knowledge;** ...but do not have love, I am nothing. (1Co.13:2)

Over forty years ago, Ron decided to follow Christ and has continued to grow not only in the knowledge but also in the likeness of Christ. Before becoming a Christian, Ron's weekends were filled with sin. When Ron became a Christian, Christ changed him to no longer desire the diversions of his past. However, other sins were harder to overcome. He sought wisdom from pastors, teachers, and conference speakers to overcome sin in his life. Some denied the possibility. Others said it was possible but could not concisely state the principles; their teachings were vague. As Ron read the Bible one day, God pointed to the beatitude:

> Blessed are those who **hunger and thirst for righteousness**, for **they will be filled.** (Mt.5:6 NIV)

Ron regularly fasted until God gave him the principles for overcoming sin. Over the years, God proved Himself faithful by providing people and literature to teach Ron these principles. The Bible teaches that the truth, when it is applied to our lives, shall set us free. Ron's life has been committed to sharing the transforming truths of God's Word in the hope that Christians will be freed from the bondage of sin and Satan. Only then can anyone experience the freedom of holiness.

www.ingramcontent.com/pod-product-compliance
Lightning Source LLC
Chambersburg PA
CBHW031641040426
42453CB00006B/178